Damaged Gods

Also by Julie Burchill

LOVE IT OR SHOVE IT

Damaged Gods

Cults and Heroes Reappraised

JULIE BURCHILL

CENTURY
London   Melbourne   Auckland   Johannesburg

'Born Again Cows' first appeared in *The Sunday Times*, February 1984, in much smaller (one thousand words) form.

Copyright © Julie Burchill 1986

All rights reserved

First published in Great Britain in 1986
by Century Hutchinson Ltd,
Brookmount House, 62–65 Chandos Place,
Covent Garden, London WC2N 4NW

British Library Cataloguing in Publication Data
Burchill, Julie
 Damaged gods : cults and heroes reappraised.
  1. Popular culture——History——20th century
 I. Title
 306   HM101

ISBN 0–7126–1140–1

Photoset by Deltatype, Ellesmere Port
Printed in Great Britain by
St Edmundsbury Press Ltd, Bury St Edmunds, Suffolk
Bound by Butler & Tanner Ltd, Frome, Somerset

Contents

Born Again Cows

'When a child is having a tantrum, you put your arms around it to calm it down' – Greenham Common person on the symbolic ringing of American nuclear warfare base, 1983.

Yes. Probably. If you don't believe in the healing powers of a good thump. But when a drooling blood-soaked maniac breaks into your house and brandishes an axe in your general direction, I suggest that *this* time your first reaction would *not* be to hug him reassuringly but to grab the nearest shotgun and blow him to kingdom come. And if we are to talk metaphors, always a grisly business, I would suggest that the American military machine has much more in common with aforementioned maniac than with afore-mentioned pouting brat.

The quote is Cowtalk, and Cowtalk is a creepy brand of language abuse rapidly becoming as ubiquitous as New-speak. On small screens and in magazines you'll find it, painting a stunningly simple picture of a world reduced to wombs and weapons, filled with gentle, intuitive, saintlike beings on the distaff side and rabid, rapacious goons on the other. It is the lot of the saints to somehow transform the goons, or else tomorrow you die. The people who tell these tales are Cows.

The working-class Cow is not so bad, tending mostly to mill about vacantly and breed overenthusiastically – depressing, but hardly calling for drastic measures. The Eighties, though, have seen the rise of a much more public-spirited Cow, the articulate, literate, media-mewing *Careerist* Cow. Boy, can she talk. And she writes books,

1

often about the singularly distasteful subject of childbirth, putting forward the Cowist line. And she haunts the corridors of Thames TV like a particularly garrulous ghost. And she puts forward Cowism as a valid philosophy – and enough is enough.

The Cow's first folly is her insistence that all human females are women. This is a popular progressive misconception. There *are* Women, but there are also Girls, and I know a couple of Broads. There are even a few Chicks left, although thankfully not many – Chicks can be wearing. The CC talks too much of Female Friendship, too; Female Friendship is fine for teenage girls and old women, both of whom are so maddening in their own way that only a similar fruitbat could tolerate it for more than five minutes, but girls in their prime should desist from sitting about in backrooms licking their wounds (sorry, 'raising their consciousnesses'). Cringeing in the ghetto is never a good idea.

There have always been Cows. Agony aunts are royal cows, displaying a bland acceptance of all (male) comers that is terrifyingly broadminded: 'Dear Claire, my boyfriend likes to put out my eyes with red hot knitting needles before we make love. Is this normal?' 'Dear Eyeless, anything that gives two people pleasure within a caring relationship is natural.' Photographic models are never Cows, they are hired for that which is most unique in a human – much more so than their *mind* – the arrangement of eyes, bones and lips, but naked models are not. Pregnant women are Cows (everyone should be pregnant once – but not twice, unless you're getting paid for it – because it really is a sobering reminder of what our lives would be like if we lived as Nature intended us, as animals, free from all harmful chemical additives; totally unautonomous, a prisoner of one's own body. Living naturally would be only slightly less unpalatable than dying slowly; one and the same, really), lined up glazed and vacant to be prodded by vets disguised as doctors. *'Don't try to understand 'em / Just throw and rope and brand 'em'* sings camp old Frankie Laine over the *Rawhide* credits, and five'll get you ten that he's singing about an ante-natal clinic.

You would not think that a feminist could possibly be a Cow; but in the Eighties, incredibly, they are in the vanguard of the mo(o)vement. Like most things people

2

believe started in the Sixties — black protest, homosexual protest, drug abuse and amusement — postwar feminism started in a small, level-headed way in the Fifties, was left off the men-orientated menu in the Sixties and finally caught on big amongst young mini-skirted media movers in the early Seventies when a number of intelligent women realized that 'alternative' men had an even slobbier attitude towards women than orthodox men. With their short skirts and long fringes, long coats and short fuses they were forever stopping the SW1 traffic with their brazenness and their banners, demanding, always demanding — abortion, equal pay, sugar and spice and all things nice. They were thrusting, always thrusting towards the right for women to tangle with men on equal terms in every walk of life and love and *win*. Beating a retreat was the last thing on their minds.

The freedom that women were supposed to have found in the Sixties largely boiled down to easy contraception and abortion; things to make life easier for men, in fact, things to make women more like chums and less like millstone medallions. But the gains of the Seventies grew out of what women wanted for themselves, drawn up from a shopping list of bitterness and old silence. They discovered that they had bulimia and anorexia, endless prescriptions for Valium and endless violence from men. They discovered, very volubly, that some men were rapists and some woman were lesbians (in the Eighties the loudest Cows in the Moovement declared that *all* normal men were rapists and *all* normal women were lesbians). They discovered that they wanted orgasms, natural childbirth and jobs as newsreaders. And by and large, they got what they wanted, if they had the guts to take it. The Seventies were a great decade for women; from the start with May Hobbs the cleaning woman to the end with Margaret Thatcher the clean-up woman, women who dared won.

Things are different now. The Eighties have seen new reasons to be tearful come to light — rising rates of alcoholism and smoking amongst women, premenstrual tension (in the Eighties women started to literally get away with murder if it could be proved they did the dirty deed when the moon was waxing and the sukebind was on the wane, as it were), sexual harrassment at work, the belated recognition of the terrible extent to which men sexually abuse their female children. Yet these problems are the concern of the medical profession, the trades unions and the organized victims of incest themselves. Organized feminists seem totally unconcerned with these very important issues.

Organized feminists today, in this country, are Cows. Whether they are the Greenham Common women, mooing and stamping in muddy rural abandon (one angry young woman with 20/20 vision and a handgun, picking off the Yanks as they arrive, would be more use to the peace movement than a million of those chanting, passive, hippie wacks, who seem to positively *glory* in their ability to lose friends and revolt people) or that Typhoid Mary of feminism, Miss Selma James, she of English Collective of Prostitutes (in which actual working prostitutes are as plentiful as raised toilet seats in convents) and Wages For Housework Campaign (ditto housewives) genius. Supporting the rights of women to be prostitutes and house-workers and little else, their politics are the politics of physical ugliness and social inadequacy, and their ideals are the most diametrically opposed to the original dream of equality that the most driven, bravest of white women that ever lived — the Suffragettes — dared to dream. Mrs Pankhurst would recognize Mrs Thatcher, who believes in women doing as men do; but she would not recognize Selma James, who believes in women doing what men want — soliciting and scrubbing.

It became a common cry from the Cow contingent in the Eighties: 'But what has Mrs Thatcher DONE for women?' Done *for* women! — these women, who called a man a Nazi if he tried to light their cigarette, suddenly wanted things DONE for them, as if they were children or mental defectives, half-people who couldn't get anywhere without having (heart) strings pulled. What Mrs Thatcher did for women was to demonstrate that if a woman had enough desire she could do what she wanted, do anything a man could do — imagine, even in the Seventies it was still in doubt. Despite the early candyfloss from her Cabinet, about how God had made woman to stay at home and not take up jobs men could be doing, it soon became clear that Mrs Thatcher did not have one traditional feminine cell in her body. She certainly did not have the traditional feminine 'moral' values that her followers so stupidly read into her; she was married to a divorced man, she had a Cabinet full of divorced men and pretty soon, thinking logically as a man would, she helped in laws that made divorce easier and maintenance harder – she believed in 'the clean break', back out to work and earn your own living, sister. Mrs Thatcher really believed that any woman worth her salt acted like a man, and those that didn't have the guts to she penalized. Ironically, the Church and the feminist groups united against the new clean-cut divorce reforms, both believing in the 'womanly' woman who is ill equipped to slog it out with the big boys on the job market.

Mrs Thatcher was the megaversion of those women who started the Seventies dubious and defensive – 'I don't believe there will be a woman Prime Minister in my lifetime' – and ended the decade with the gloves off. At the end of the Seventies the feminist road forked, and you had to decide, it seemed – REV UP OR DROP OUT. Women with marketable assets decided that success was the best sex-war revenge and set about utilizing themselves in the Eighties. In the tradition of the Jongian novel and the Gurley magazine, sisterhood went selfish. The struggle went soapy and glossy – SexCareerMoney, the three things became inseparable in a certain kind of solitary, go-getting feminism, and became a natural for the rags to Rykiel form of so much modern entertainment. Sob sisters who became famous advising other women on how to pull themselves together and get the most from their only life, their real life, suddenly seemed to think that if you couldn't get them to do this you may as well add more grist to the mill of that most chronic of female complaints – escapism – and make a mint. YOU HAD YOUR CHANCE, was their attitude, NOW BUY MY TRASH. Even Zoe Fairbairns made the blockbuster Book Club big league, though more in the mode of *Roots* than *Dallas*. Erin Pizzey went the furthest; she not only took to writing romances like a duck to orange sauce but left her Women's Refuge, said that some women *liked* being thumped, married a swarthy young Semitic stud and decamped for America. Not so much revisionism as amnesia.

Women became big bucks in the Eighties, and women who had previously been products became their own best promoters and publicists. Women of forty and fifty, still beautiful, provided the best argument — the *only* argument — against newly sighted 'ageism' by being photographed in lots of leotards and lying through their perfectly capped teeth that any woman could look the same if she earned fifty thousand dollars a week — sorry, *exercised*. Joan Collins — the oldest sex symbol since Mae West — and Raquel Welch — who proved to be as intelligent as she was beautiful, no mean feat — worked their tushes off promoting their beauty books; the best bit came when Raquel Welch, appearing on 'Good Morning America' to shift some units, told an astonished nation to leave Nicaragua alone. There were other, smaller rebellions; ex-starlets like Britt Ekland became notorious for using young studs as rich old men had used them when *they* were starlets. They wore their boys as pure decoration, something shiny on the arm — like a diamond bracelet, only cheaper and with less conversation.

Advertising, the last bastion of the Pure Cow — not the Career Cow, or the Politicow, but the pre-feminist girdle-wearing husband-worshipping smallscreen housewife — finally fell to female mobility in the Eighties, largely due to the impatient influence of all those painfully intelligent, cynical, coke-sniffing Seventies graduate girls who saw no other option but to go into advertising — the perfect joke job for a life that was one long black joke. There were adverts for washing powder stressing how it would give you time 'to do what you *want* to do' (assuming, for the first time, that women *didn't want to do housework*) and adverts for washing machines which ridiculed men: 'So simple a man can use it.'

They were adverts aimed at the Cosmo Girl grown up, married yet still mobile. The *Cosmopolitan* of the Eighties stresses career, Spartan vegetable 'cleansing' diets and cocksucking — what more could any girl want? It flirted very briefly with the so-called New Celibacy — which all boiled down to half a dozen hacks who had given each other herpes and were thus cheesed off/off sex, and wrote about it a lot — but was soon back to health, with physical love scoring almost as high as fiscal shove. It became very easy to make fun of *Cosmopolitan* in the Seventies and Eighties, especially if you were young and hip and took your freedom for granted; but when all is said and done, despite its dated glibness and old-fashioned hi-tech look — *Cosmopolitan* was a Good Thing, stressing work and sex in a complimentary style in a way no girls' magazine had done before or since; in a way men's magazines had been doing for ever, it seemed. In the best possible way, *Cosmopolitan* was not so much a magazine for women in general as for *male impersonators*. It realized that women did not have penis envy, but Access envy; that women did not want to *be* men, but would be pleased to adopt protective masculine colouring in order to reap the material rewards that we are all brought up to believe bring happiness. And maybe they do.

Occasionally *Cosmo* went too far; they fell hard for female bodybuilders, updated Diane Arbus people with the cod-feminist spiel, pathetic New York City women in their tacky late twenties who had been things like 'students of French language and civilization', 'sculptresses' and 'ceramicists' — those modern things that really stupid, phoney girls always do, the sort that used to be in mime and modern ballet — until they decided that if they only had one life to lead, they may as well lead it as their own masterpiece. With an idiot narcissism previously only found in male homosexualists they expose the bulging veins on their biceps with the bonehead boastfulness of a bumpkin showing a freak giant marrow at a country show, seemingly unaware that THESE THINGS are attached to them. Take into consideration the photographer Robert Mapplethorpe's interest in ladies of the might, and your prejudices are confirmed; these women are walking Art Fag jokes, fashioned to confirm all fags' worst fears about women — grotesque, castrating — and thus justify their odd sex preferences — justifiable homocide.

Muscle aside, *Cosmopolitan* had glimpsed the truth; that a woman who looks like a girl and thinks like a man is the

7

best sort, the most enjoyable to be and the most pleasurable to have and to hold. It is an odd modern paradox that the girls who admire and ape the trad male values the most — ambition, hedonism — appear the most attractive and feminine while the women who admire 'female' virtues tend to look like men — flat chests, facial hair and all.

To the Cow, the Cosmo Girl is worse than a — boo, hiss — *man*. Hell hath no fury like a wallflower with a Sociology degree, and the glamour ambitions of the CG really get on the Cow's tits — or they would, if she had any. Spurned by society (i.e. not chased by men) the Politicow considers any achievement achieved in said society worthless, and derides ambitious or successful women incessantly. 'Businesswomen have contempt for their mothers,' says Selma James, 'if they don't work' — and quite right, too. The crackpot logic of the Politicows thus leads them to idealize and speak out for women who have accomplished nothing in the race — notably those two most treacherous parodies of the human female, the prostitute and the housewife.

The organized feminists of the Eighties do not call for easier abortion or more equal pay, probably because they neither work nor fuck — what a life! Instead they bray for 'Wages For Housework', 'Wages Due Lesbians' and — wait for it — 'Wages Due Black Lesbians', the names of these sub-groups being so ill thought out that they imply that black lesbians should receive a wage simply for *being* black lesbians. But even *more* astonishing than the picture of the housewife as a struggling sister with a feather duster in one hand and an Armalite in the other was the amazing triple-think that allowed these people who called themselves feminists to take up the cause of the prostitute.

The idea that a man and a woman might love each other, completely, despite all the distance and history between them, scares the Politicows stiff. And so they like to pretend that prostitution is the only 'honest' form of heterosex. In their illness and their ugliness they do not seem to understand what it is to feel attraction, and to attract; they deliberately choose to miss the *purity* of the transaction of unfinanced sex, the free exchange of bodies for at least pleasure and at best the ecstasy that transforms life. The early feminists dreamed of free love; these drabs demonstrate in favour of shop-soiled sex for sale, and glory in the cheapening of the most potentially honest, rawest and most awe-inspiring experience available to a human being that prostitution entails. To bring something as humdrum and modern as money into this most mysterious, moral part of life, to make physical love a JOB – this makes prostitution an obscenity almost as much as the slimy condoms which litter children's playgrounds in the districts frequented by the Quislings of the quim.

The sheer idea that prostitution could *ever* be compatible with the struggle for truth, justice and the feminist-socialist way! Apart from making the lives of the (mostly working-class) residents of the areas in which they ply their poxy trade even more depressing (in more than one part of South London tenants keep baseball bats and buckets of water by their front doors in order to drive away both the monstrous, moronic regiments who fornicate in their front gardens and the men who come banging on the door looking for them), prostitution is the supreme triumph of capitalism – or it was, until the surrogate baby episode. Even the means by which the race reproduces itself can bought and sold.

Worst of all, prostitution reinforces all the old dumb clichés about women's sexuality; that they are not built to enjoy sex and are little more than walking masturbation aids, things to be DONE TO, things so sensually null and void that they have to be *paid* to indulge in fornication, that women can be had, bought, as often as not sold by one man to another; in formerly respectable districts that prostitutes have swamped and ghettoized, all women are approached by men as if they are for hire. When the sex war is won prostitutes should be shot as collaborators for their terrible betrayal of all women, for the moral tarring and feathering they give indigenous women who have the bad luck to live in what they make their humping ground. No wonder lesbians are so copious and vocal in the Eighties prostitution lobby; lesbians loathe heterosexuality, and if anything is conducive to bad heterosexual relationships prostitution is. Sweep the strange desires under the carpet, under the counter; have the nice sex with the wife, the nasty sex with the whore. Even more than men, it is prostitutes who keep the double standard alive and kicking and sick.

The slogans of these women are incredible; they make the epigrams of the Chelsea Shed Boys sound like the Sermon on the Mount. KILL MEN – THEY'RE KILLING US. WE ARE ALL PROSTITUTES. ALL MEN ARE RAPISTS. While less than accurate, these slogans certainly serve their function – as a sort of cerebral Horlicks to send the Politicows to sleep easy each night, secure in the knowledge that the problem is too big to be tackled. If no one is innocent, then no one is guilty. Thus the Politicows can justify their endless cud-chewing and nothing doing.

The tragedy is that feminism, real, active, practical organized feminism, is still NEEDED; the world is far from post-feminist. Though the women who are worthy of our concern are not the tax-free tarts of Tooting Bec but the 75 million plus women of the African continent and the Arabian peninsula currently suffering the life-long after effects of the ritual genital mutilation known politely and pathetically as 'female circumcision' (as if the butchery was in some way comparable to the beautifying cosmetic surgery practised on baby Jews) but which is actually nothing less than female castration – the effective neutering of women. It is as though some white trader threw in a Barbie Doll with the glass beads he dazzled the natives with long ago, and ever since they have been doing their best to make females of their type resemble this ugly, Godforsaken image of woman – no clitoris, and for most of the time no sexual opening. The disgusting internal illnesses and the high infant mortality rate which follow in the wake of this desecration are considered less important than the Arab/African right to pursue their 'tradition' – but as wised-up Western women should know, 'tradition' mostly means bad habits born of ignorance. It is the white Western male tradition to beat wives; it is the European tradition to persecute Jews. So what? Why should they be continued? And bad habits born of superstition: in Upper Volta and Mali, it is believed that a man will die if his penis comes into contact with the clitoris, hence the female is castrated. We do no favour to African men, let alone their female victims, to encourage them in or to respect this hokum; the longer they believe these things, the longer their countries will be the backward hell holes they are today. The fact is that female castration is nothing more − not a cultural tradition or a health move − than a crusade to terrorize women out of sexual desire by the stupid, sexually ignorant men of the Afro/Arab world.

Where are the Western feminists who are so loud in defence of housewives and hookers when these tortured creatures need their support? The American, Frances Hosken, who for years has been trying to mobilize opinion against these atrocities in tradition's clothing, said in the late Seventies, 'International agencies, as well as charitable and church groups and family planning organizations working in Africa have engaged in a conspiracy of silence . . . as a result, those African women who are working for a change in their own countries have been completely isolated or ignored.' Incredibly, what with everything else they have to worry about in their countries of origin, women such as Dr Fatima Mahmoud of the Sudan, Mehani Selah of the South Yemen Ministry of Health and Awa Thiam of Senegal, and organizations such as the Voltaic Women's Federation and the Somali Women's Democratic Organization, campaign against female castration. It is to the everlasting shame of Western women's groups that their considerable voices are never heard on this most crucial of crucifying issues.

Since oil wealth, it has been the practice of rich Arabs to have their daughters castrated in the cool closed surgeries of the West. Denmark, Sweden and Norway, always in the vanguard of civilization, have banned the neutering of women on their soil, but in London several thousand clitori come annually under the Harley Street hammer. Valerie Wise, loud leader of the Greater London Council's Women's Committee, could be found in early 1985 protesting against, if you please, the desire of some soft-centred promoter to hand out 1500 red roses to female members of a St Valentine's Day bash at the Festival Hall on the gounds that it was 'sexist', being 'old-fashioned behaviour'. Oh no, surely it was a *tradition*, and a pretty harmless one at that − ask any woman if she'd prefer a red rose or her clitoris cut off and five'll get you ten that the bloom wins out over the blade every time.

The GLC Women's Committee would be hardpushed, too, to excuse themselves on their lack of action on the grounds that what goes on outside London is no concern of theirs, and that while these Arabs may use London clinics they are citizens of other sovereign states. It is well known that the GLC leaders consider all men from Tralee to Tripoli their brothers' keepers, and constantly pass comment on the captivity of one man in South Africa. Why then have they never said anything about the castrating of millions of women in the surrounding black African countries? Of course this is a rhetorical question, and easily answered; it is because of the inverted ethnocentricity of white socialists and feminists, who believe that anything done by white men to women − even giving them roses − is 'bad' while anything done by black men to women − including gouging out their genitalia − is 'good', 'natural', 'traditional'. 'Tradition' means nothing more than 'This is what we have done for a long time'; it is not its own justification, and it cannot be a justification for cruelty and ignorance in Africa any more than it can be in England.

In the 1980s a new (primary) school of thought crept into what was left of organized English feminism: that somehow things had been better in the past for women. The Extended Family! Before Tower Blocks! Of course, feminists coming from the caste they do they never have a chance to experience the joys of your actual Ext Fam; but try asking any skint young working-class married woman who has been forced to embark upon her voyage of conjugal bliss living with her mother-in-law, and she'll paint you a vivid enough picture. And the past being a foreign country, it was not long before you could hear feminists claiming that Western women, despite − or perhaps *because of* − their leisure and lipstick, careers and contraceptives, had much worse lives than women in the underdeveloped countries.

Imagine! The orphaned hippie dream of rural idylls and communes and India and back(ward) to nature, man, had found a belated des. res. within a movement that could ill afford its slothful, fuzzy-minded presence and pretence. It was O.K. for the hippies to play with those silly notions; as

12

white, mostly middle-class men they had all they needed and could afford to play dumb and slum in cultural cul de sacs. But women have not yet got one quarter of what is rightfully theirs, and for them to indulge in these folksy fictions is a terrible waste of time and energy. This hippie hi-jack of feminism led to what is the most distressing development to date in the annals of Cowism: the birth of the Born Again Cow, a nice, intelligent, arty career girl who took a wrong turning and had a screw come loose.

The most prominent and promotable of these was probably Germaine Greer, who really does believe that a woman living in a country which contains bride-burning has a better life than a woman living in a country which contains *Bride* magazine. Miss Greer has taken against all things Western — except money and the media — and pursued the Pill with the savage self-righteousness of Senator McCarthy on the trail of a Stalinist starlet. In advising the use of the withdrawal method and the condom to young people (*The Face*, 1984), the most sterile, anti-sensual forms of contraception known to man — yuk! keep your nasty sperm to yourself!: saying no to a man is more intimate than expecting him to take a bath with his raincoat on — she revealed herself as a true cowering Catholic at heart, a guilty party long past it. Her eccentricity was confirmed when she stated that childbrirth may be 'more pleasurable than an orgasm' — *well!* One wonders if Miss Greer has ever *had* an orgasm, if she can in all honesty say this. She has certainly never had a child; only a sterile woman could have such unrealistic, romantic ideas about childbirth, and advocate non-stop breeding as a cure to all known (Third) world ills. It is quite possible, judging from her recent writings, to imagine that Miss Greer never really liked sex at all but *pretended* to so that men would talk to her, as so many plain, intelligent girls did during the 1960s.

Although the Eighties have seen certain wild crooner girls — Christine Hynde, Poly Styrene, Sandie Shaw, Annie Lennox — renounce their wild ways and go on to have babies and become Buddhist housewives, most BACs are literary. The novelist Susan Hill is a genteel sort of BAC; never was so much fruit preserved by so few for so many. Angela Carter is a BAC with an endless bookful of bedtime stories, turning women into babies by writing fairytales for them. And in 1984 The Women's Press published *The Subversive Stitch*, a celebration of women's heritage – in embroidery. Since the first organized female anger, feminism had come full circle. We need women who condone embroidery – or housework, or prostitution – like we need blacks who condone shoe-shining and slavery.

The Born Again Cow is much worse than her Seventies precursor the Earth Mother, because the Earth Mother always had the inclination and as she went to seed in the outer suburbs of youth it really wasn't a matter of great concern – her ankles had never been anything to write home about, anyway. But you can't tell a BAC until she creeps up on you and starts whispering sweet nothings in your ear. Born Again Cows don't just run quietly to seed like Earth Mothers but go around advocating Cowdom for all women, girls and broads. Don't listen; the way forward is not as the BAC believes but as the suffragettes started. In *demanding*, and *getting* – the Vote, work, divorce, sex, love, money; surely this life, now, in the West, the confused, frantic, competitive, neurotic West, is the nearest thing to heaven women have ever known – not in *retreating* into wholefoods and womb workshops. It is true that women have been horribly oppressed, hideously persecuted, burnt as witches, reviled as bitches, raped as itches – but there are so many wonderful men in the world, and so many wonderful women, and so many dumb men, and so many dumb women. To try and sort them into two different sorts of human being simply by virtue of what they grow between their legs is as logical as trying to sort them into two different sorts of human being by virtue of what they grow on the heads – blond or brunette, curly or straight, short or long. You can change your hair, and for a slightly higher price you can change your genitalia, but it doesn't change your *self*. People are people; they are sub-divided into men and women on the dotted line, but not at heart.

Be on your guard, and the next time some cosy, dozy bovine type tells you that because you're a female human you are automatically intuitive, nurturing and sensitive, and that men are beasts to be calmed down and civilized by little you, kick her in the thick shins and run. A cow is a cow is a cow, and it behooves a cow to act like a cow; stand in a little field, chew a little cud, breed, watch the world go by and wait to be slaughtered. But that's not the life for you, girl. Beware the BAC and her glad tidings that women are passive angels and men are aggressive fiends; it is the poisonous, restricting message of the pre-feminist Dark Ages, and this new hype with woman as the angel of the hearth (or airbase) is no less malign coming from a woman than from a − boo, hiss − man.

The Method Rhythm

What we in the West call the Third World is really the Real World, in which real things happen, in which real wars are fought, in which there is real room for real development and disaster. The white world in general, and the American-speaking world in particular, is more or less a Toy World, a place often resembling a massive playpen wherein the occupants distract themselves from their own painful powerlessness with a parade of trends, fads and entertainments, dummies to suck thrown into the cot-cage for the dummies within.

We have toy traumas; the white world has 'angst', against the real world's anguish, the real world's agony. Angst is what people have when they have no real troubles; as the over-refined, soft diet damages the body, the over-refined soft life damages the soul. And we have toy wars; and the Toy War at its most blatant is the one fought out within the battlefield of the Generation Gap.

They are understandable, these boy toy soldiers, even while they are ridiculous; respectable grown-up life is, on the whole, a wretched affair – married to a mortgage, living through the TV. Adolescence is a time of panic as the life sentence approaches at full speed along the tracks of your teens – a second babyhood full of tantrums and resistance. And in the postwar white world, the showbrat world, it is quite likely that one may be spotted by a tastemaker while having one's tantrum, and then one may hone it and polish it and make it one's art, and meet influential media people who will help you *make a living* out of it, a bigger, brighter living out of your tantrum than your

16

parents could ever make out of their docility, maybe for just one season, maybe well into your adult life. This is the age of the tantrum — or it *was*, until very recently . . .

Each and every chapel in the parade of wayward youth leans towards one or other of the Eternal Attitudes — Bohemian or Hooligan. The Teds were militant Hooligan. The Method Actors and the Angry Young Men were both Bohemian, though their pretensions towards the mantle of primitive genius required sporadic outbreaks of the Hooligan. Likewise the Kitchen Sink Heroes had frustrated Bohemian tendencies and expressed their frustration in a Hooligan manner (sicking up on the mother-in-law's carpet — acts of Hooliganism on the part of *frustrated* Bohemians served to draw attention to their spurned sensitivity).

Skinheads were fanatical Hooligan — they should have carried Tonik prayer mats and bowed down in the direction of the nearest casualty ward five times a day. Hippie was credit card Bohemia. Anything on a motorbike — Rockers, Greasers, Hell's Angels — was Hooligan, though *not necessarily* something on a scooter. Mods, though they ended up as extremist Hooligan — blood on the sand! — had their roots in aesthetic Bohemia, noble beginnings that made Modernism a joy forever. Likewise Punk had its origins in art school Bohemia but had to incorporate a strong Hooligan element just to keep the rhetoric afloat.

While not all of these amalgamated action boys were fully paid up members of a youth cult — John Osborne probably never hung out on a street corner with a mob of angry young playwrights — I'm sure we would have heard about it if he had — all were collective expressions of discontents and aspirations manifested in style and action. All were small cogs in the cult of youth, a modern invention which, like most contemporary phenomena, came complete with its own built-in obsolescence and has now had its day.

The golden years of teenage can be dated from the unconditional surrender of Japan in 1945 to the unconditional surrender of the British people in 1979 and the election of Mrs Thatcher. Angry young attitudes are rare when times are truly tough; Punk flourished under the benign leadership and balmy economic climate of Callaghan's Britain. Mrs Thatcher would have legislated against it.

Unlike the Hooligans (which is what they were as well as what they were called) of late Victorian England — noted for their donkey fringes, bellbottoms and blunt instruments — the postwar cults of youth sometimes aspired to something more than making a few dishonest bob and beating the gang in the next neighbourhood to a bloody Victorian pulp. (Sometimes.) Before the war teenagers were little adults, trainee drones, second-class citizens. After the war they achieved sovereign status; they became a market. The early steps to sovereignty were made by annexation — once the Teds had claimed something as their own nobody else wanted it. It was tainted.

In 1950, as a whoop of abandon after wartime austerity, a Savile Row tailor revived the Edwardian Dandy look – long, narrow-lapelled jacket, white, cutaway shirt with a Windsor-knot tie, narrow trousers (though not drainpipes) and rococo waistcoat. Now, for the first time, young proles were able to pick up on the tastes of the toffs – from 1945 to 1950 the average wage of teenagers had increased at twice the rate of the adult wage. The look spread like an epidemic throughout the seminal Teds of South London and by 1954 the *Daily Mirror* was carrying front page news of upper-class males purging their wardrobes of Edwardian suits, desperate not to be mistaken for one of those Teddy fellows, unloading their Edwardian chic onto markets where it could be picked up easily and cheaply by new recruits.

The first Ted murder had happened the year before on Clapham Common when Michael Davies, a Ted, was charmingly referred to as a 'flash cunt' by a passing civilian. The civilian wound up dead and Michael Davies was convicted for what Fleet Street called 'The First Teddy Boy Killing', which in itself promised more to come. The Teds were very touchy about their appearance. Apart from the extra pounds in their pocket, it was all they had. Being a Ted meant status, a source of pride and sent out a signal to the rest of the world — 'Shove it up your ass', basically. The Teds did not make the Edwardian suit — circa Savile Row

1950, that is – their own merely by making it unacceptable garb for any aristocratic follower of fashion by virtue of Ted behaviour and reputation alone. The Teds added their own amendments, they proletarianized the look, projecting their own fancies and fantasies onto it. Narrow trousers became drainpipes – antithesis of the baggy respectability of the de-mob suit. Fluorescent colours were introduced – two fingers up at ration-card austerity and a knowing nod of acknowledgement towards pimpdom. The jacket became straighter, losing the waisted look and gaining a satin, velvet or moleskin collar.

They looked like Technicolor undertakers, real death merchants, which was only partly a joke.

The tie with the Windsor-knot became bootlaced, Westernized – Teds picked up on the bootlace tie from cowboy films. They were not so impeccably British that they could resist the howling sirens of Hollywood. In Westerns the bootlace tie was the prerogative of the riverboat gambler, the Mississippi spiv who was invariably urban and urbane, hedonistic and quick-witted (everything the Teds coveted – they managed the urban and hedonistic parts) rather than rural, hard-working and decent. Teds were not at all decent. Teds gloried in their indecency. The supreme ironic amendment the Teds made to the Edwardian suit was, après Elvis, le blue – or pink or green or aubergine – suede shoe, with a whole lot of crepe sole. More than any other youth cult, Teds were identified and identified themselves with rock and roll. Yet while in the cracker belt of the United States of America rock and roll records were being burned, condemned to eternal bonfires as 'race music', in Merry Olde England the Teds, self-proclaimed apostles of rock and roll, were trashing anything on the wrong side of beige.

The behaviour of the champions of the jungle beat was always such that it made the Ku Klux Klan look like closet pinkos. In the *Daily Express* Giles cartoons depicted Teds joining forces with Beatniks to attack bowler-hatted city gents – a more unlikely alliance or target is hard to imagine. Teds liked attacking bus conductors (who tended to goad the Teds into violence by asking them provocative questions such as, May I have your fare please?) and youth clubs (even the few youth clubs that admitted Teds were not safe as they rarely lived up to the demanding standards that the Teds expected from their pleasure palaces) and each other. But, above and beyond all these moving targets that the Teds had known and assaulted, their main motivation for bloodshed was race.

Ted attacks on Cypriot café owners and blacks eventually culminated in the 1958 race riots in Nottingham and Notting Hill. Many working-class adults joined the riots once they were under way, but they were started by the boys in blue suede shoes. The nine unskilled working-class adolescents accused of starting the Notting Hill riots, each sentenced to four years' imprisonment, were all Teds.

The first impression of the Teds is that they were narcissistic Neanderthals, the cult of youth's cave-dwellers, fossils from a primitive era (the Grease Age?). On closer examination they appear horribly contemporary – a brutal, bitter by-product of the postwar rediscovery of class, and more specifically of lower-class powerlessness.

The Blitz Spirit, despite the revisionists, was no mere myth. The Teds spent their formative years in the nearest that Britain will ever come to a classless society. A society without class is only possible when bombs – never the greatest respecter of breeding – are raining on one's nation. After the war no one could stop the same old caste system roaring back in – certainly not Mr Attlee with his humble gifts of a bottle of free milk and a pair of National Health specs. The Teds had their expectations unrealistically raised by growing up British during World War II. The supreme irony is that they would have made very good Nazis.

Pre-sovereignty teenagers were little adults. After sovereignty they were big babies, and they were begat by the Method. The Method turned adolescent angst into an art form. By its very nature there is nothing specific about angst, it is based upon nothing of any substance, and after the Method teenagers, more than anything, demanded the right to whinge.

The Actor's Studio – the Method's Mecca, USA – was a white building on New York City's West Forty-Fourth

Street with lavatories labelled 'Romeo' and 'Juliet'. It was founded by Lee Strasberg on the ideas of Konstantin Stanislavsky, who had 'evolved' a 'new' 'method' of acting in which the actor, essentially, did not merely *play* parts but *became* the part, drawing on his own natural resources and experiences to create a character rather than portray one. An invitation to self-delusion, the Method offered an opportunity for actors never to have to admit that they were wearing masks, blurring the line between fantasy and reality – ciphers no more! – an attraction that was impossible to resist, both to themselves and their constituency. The Method and its practitioners had a more profound effect on white Western teenagers in the Fifties than even rock and roll. The Method achieved the ultimate postwar showbusiness dream – it was bigger than Elvis. James Dean died for a million adolescent sins.

James Bridges: 'I was in college when Jimmy died. Some guy came running into the theatre where we were working on scenery and started shouting "Hey, you all, Jimmy Dean is dead", and we all went to a place called the Polaram and bought lots of booze and got really plastered. We just couldn't stand it. We went down to the river and built a fire and had our own wake. I made an Academy Award out of mud and put it in the fire. Then we had a mud fight and started chanting "Give us a sign, give us a sign", and we all had our shirts off. A dog barked on the side of the hill, so then we knew he was there.'

In the first year after Mr Dean's death Warner Brothers received more than fifty thousand letters to the late lamented James. Fully paid up members of various unofficial fan clubs – 'Dean's Teens', 'Dedicated Deans', 'James Dean's Memorial Club' and 'Lest We Forget' – numbered amost *four million* in the US alone. Many fans refused to believe he was dead. A one-shot magazine called *Jimmy Dean Returns* sold half a million copies at 35 cents a time – more than twice the price of most movie magazines of the time. Those who believed he was still alive went along with the theory that he was hidden in an institution, hideously mutilated, crippled and insane. One member of the James Dean Death Club – whose party line, perversely, insisted he was not dead at all — said in 1956, 'We know where he is and we've got a lookout there. They keep all the shades down but one night we got close enough to look through a tear in the blind and we saw him sitting there swathed in bandages. He acted like he wasn't quite right in his mind.'

An aspiring actor called Thomas Pittman killed himself by crashing his car into a tree, enabling him to join his hero at that great drive-in in the sky. In Germany two teenage girls committed suicide, leaving a letter to their parents which said, 'This was the anniversary of the day Jimmy died and life is intolerable without him.'

The Man Who Started It All! The First Teenager!

James Dean was the Peter Pan of pop culture, dying — impaled on the wheel of his Porsche, an act of accidental suicide — rather than leave Never-Never Land. His death was the only possible punchline in his life. It breathed life into the myth and made his films monuments to the legend.

The New Republic said, 'It is significant that there is little interest in what Dean might have gone on to do if he had not died. His death was a fitting culmination to his life, senseless, but justified by the story.'

So what was the story? To de-code the cultural significance of James Dean it is necessary to go back to the genesis of youthdom, to the days when teenage culture was just another colonial outpost of the adult empire.

Warner Brothers bought *Rebel Without a Cause*, a book by Doctor Robert M. Lindner, in 1946. Almost inevitably, *Rebel Without a Cause* — a story, *the* story of juvenile delinquency in the Fifties, a time when being a JD was a social disease, caused by society and curable by therapy — was written by a quack.

But juvenile delinquency did not make for a hot property in 1946. Says William Orr, a Warners' executive of the time, 'When I did the original screen test for *Rebel Without a Cause* in 1947 I finally gave the leading role to Marlon Brando. The script wasn't even finished, but I knew I was looking for a sensitive, unusual young man and everybody kept telling me, "You must see Marlo Brinden, or Maylin Brandin . . . ". No one was really quite sure *what* his name was. Someone said he was running an elevator in Macy's, and another person told us that the night before he had swum across the reservoir in Central Park. We kept hearing these great stories about him and finally found out who his agent was and she came in and said, 'Oh, Marlon isn't interested in getting into pictures at all.' So I looked at her and said, 'Wait a minute, you're in my office aren't you?' After we established that she was there and I was there and Marlon wasn't interested in pictures she set up an interview for us. When he came for his screen test he didn't say a word. He just sat there tearing up an envelope into little pieces. So I figured he was a genius and signed him. I got back to California, read the script and it *schtunk*. So we never made the picture, nor did we exercise Brando's contract.'

By 1954, however, after seven years in Warners' bottom drawer, juvenile delinquency was a cause for cultural concern. More specifically, with both *The Wild One* and *Blackboard Jungle* out on release, both made on a tiny budget and both bringing home huge amounts of Bacobits, juvenile delinquency was *hot*. *Blackboard Jungle* was a cluttered forerunner of what was to come − it was a film about an angry young mob. Rebellion, neurosis, pre-therapy bile − all multiplied though not magnified. Rather, it is all diluted (the focus of the film is idealistic school ma'am Glenn Ford). Hollywood soon came to accept that too many neurotic boys spoiled the angst; with *Blackboard Jungle* you could riot in the aisle but there was nothing there to take home to your bedroom and brood about − the private allotment where teen dreams are cultivated.

In *The Wild One* a gang of bikers take over and terrorize a small town. Like many Method films, the lead role is that of a child in male impersonator's clothing. Marlon Brando does not play a biker, a common misapprehension; he plays a child. When he is asked 'What are you rebelling against?' he famously quips, 'What have you got?', elevating the mindless tantrum to new heights of glory, metaphorically biting the top off his rattle.

For the most part in Method films, Method male leads play parts − create characters! − who are self-centred, irresponsible and blameless. In short, they play *children*. Pauline Kael in *I Lost It at the Movies* says, 'The mixed-up kid has evolved from the Depression hero, but the explanation from the Thirties (poverty did this) no longer works, and the refinement of it in *On the Waterfront* (corruption did this) didn't work. It gives way in *East of Eden* to something even more facile and fashionable: the psychiatric explanation (lack of love did this). The concept of Terry in *On the Waterfront* was a little behind the times. He was posited as heroic because he acted for the social good. Cal, in *East of Eden*, is the hero simply and completely because of his *need*, and his frenzied behaviour, the "bad" things that he does.'

Rebel Without a Cause took this infantication process even further. Come the hour, come the crazy mixed-up kid. Dean craved love, affection, understanding, but most of all – he craved therapy. The Fifties was the dawn of the age of consumer durables. While the parents were encouraged to yearn for a new car, a refrigerator or TV set, their brats were encouraged to covet spot cream, race records and psychiatric help. The director and producer of *Rebel Without a Cause*, Nicholas Ray and David Wisebart, personally screen tested all applicants for the film's initial casting call, asking questions like, 'How do you get along with your mother?' Margaret O'Brien, testing for the role of Judy, was shown the door for saying she loved her parents.

The world of *Rebel Without a Cause* is a place where child abuse is when Dad refuses to let Junior have the keys to the car.

Stewart Stern had the final say on the screenplay and wrote in his character analysis of the male lead, 'Jim Stark (James Dean): The angry victim and the result. At seventeen, he is filled with confusion about his role in life. Because of his 'nowhere' father, he does not know how to be a man. Because of his wounding mother, he anticipates destruction in all women. And yet he wants to find a girl who will be willing to receive his tenderness.'

The film opens with James Dean roaring drunk in the gutter playing with a little wind-up chimpanzee doll – something an intelligent four-year-old might donate to the Oxfam shop because he had outgrown it – putting his pet monkey to bed under a scrap of newspaper before curling up into a fetal position and joining the toy chimp in the land of Nod. The cops arrive with sirens screaming to give Jim his early morning call, carting him off to the station where the co-stars have already arrived. Plato (Sal Mineo) has been picked up for shooting a litter of puppies – a cry from the heart because his mother has stopped him going to see his analyst (the bitch). Judy (Natalie Wood) has been picked up for streetwalking – *her* beef with humanity being that her father refuses to neck with her.

It is soon clear that these young people are *not at fault*. They are entirely blameless. It is all their parents' fault. Jim's trouble is that he has a weak father and a strong mother. Judy's trouble is that she has a strong father and a weak mother. Plato's trouble is that his parents are divorced. The cops realize that society is to blame and are so big-hearted that they allow Jim to keep his toy chimp (he becomes almost psychotic at the thought it might be taken away from him and put into care).

Early in the film Jim Stark tells his meek and mild father off because Dad was about to clear up the mess he made by stupidly dropping a tray of nosh. 'Let her see it. LET HER SEE IT!' Jim Stark shrieks passionately, referring to his Mom. Was there ever masculinity in such a state of crisis as *this*? The rampant MOMism of the film is staggering. MOMism was very big in Fifties America; shrinks of every description suddenly discovered that every mal-content, hoodlum, junkie, pervert, psychopath, failure, etc, all had one thing in common. In their backgrounds was a MOTHER! It was all *her* fault! MOMism, like the Method itself, meant never having to say that you were guilty.

Mom was a castrator, emasculating men, cutting off their sexparts for earrings, waving them off to the humble office each and every morning when, of course, if not for these penis-envying Amazons of the suburbs, the little man would be out killing a herd of buffalo with his bare hands and roasting Red Indians. Like these things do, it filtered down through the concerned murmurings of academics and intellectuals through the media to its (and every-thing's) final resting place – the situation comedy. They were soon bursting at the seams with cowed American Manhood in Retreat – short-assed hubby screwing up everything he puts his hand to, with the intimidating bulk of the becurlered, meat cleaver-totting little woman towering over him.

Rebel Without a Cause contained some of the most hysterical MOMism ever, an inevitable by-product of the infantication process of the Method. It showed James Dean visibly breaking out in a cold sweat if the women weren't kept down there with the Negroes. Plato, Judy and Jim hole up in a deserted mansion and play house, a scene so coy it makes Barbara Cartland read like *Last Exit To Brooklyn*. 'I'm happy here,' swoons Plato. 'I wish we could stay here forever.' Alas, it is only a wonderful dream. Plato falls asleep and Jim and Judy go off to explore. When Plato awakes he finds himself surrounded by two large gentlemen who answer to the names of Crunch and Goon, who are looking for Jim who they believe grassed on them to the law.

Hysterical at the thought that he has been deserted by Jim and Judy, the nutty Plato runs off and hides in the Griffith Park Observatory with his Mom's .45. The police arrive and surround the building while Jim goes inside to disarm Plato — with love — and coax him out. This he does, but no sooner is Plato out in the land of the living than he is gunned down by a gung-ho cop.

The climax of the film demonstrates how the Method movies were not above getting cold feet and copping out for commercial considerations. The end of *Rebel Without a Cause* has a reconciliation scene that could rot your teeth. Jim tears himself away from Plato's still warm young corpse (it is ironic that the LAPD cooperated with the making of *Rebel Without a Cause* while the NYPD refused to help in the production of *Blackboard Jungle* — ironic because it is only in *Rebel Without a Cause* that the police gun down an unarmed, misunderstood young lad), gets down on his bended knees and hugs his father's legs — 'Help me!' — and then takes Judy home to tea with his parents after his 'nowhere' father has finally stood up to his 'wounding' mother with a look that could curdle milk.

The Wild One was similarly watered down. In *J. D. Films* by Mark Thomas McGee and R. J. Robertson the authors assert, 'Producer Stanley Kramer's original intention [in *The Wild One*] had been to show the intolerance of middle

America to anyone who varied from the norm. A concept too unsettling for the censors to accept. Emphasis was, instead, shifted to the violence of the gang, and attempts to justify their hostility were blunted. The hypocrisies of the businessmen were similarly downplayed.'

These films attempt to de-criminalize juvenile delinquency. Yet there is a certain ambiguity about this. In a startling number of the films of Marlon Brando's — *The Wild One* (1954), *On the Waterfront* (1954), *One-Eyed Jacks* (1961). *The Chase* (1966), *The Apaloosa* (1966) — the character played — created! — by Brando is given a spectacular beating, bad children having to be punished, despite Spock.

James Dean, of course, got the death penalty.

Rebel Without a Cause was originally seen by Warner Brothers as a B movie, very much a treading water project for their rising young star prior to shooting *The Left-Handed Gun* and *Somebody Up There Likes Me* (both roles — Jesse James and Rocky Graziano — were inherited by Paul Newman). The film achieved such phenomenal success for two reasons. It went on release — timing as exquisite as timing gets — just four days after James Dean was impaled on his steering wheel on Highway 466 and it captured perfectly the mood of the Method.

Its boom at the box office and its primetime slot in popular folklore were always assured.

More than any other cultural artefact the film proved that the cult of teenage, with its blameless devotion and rites of angry young attitudes, was not a bridge between childhood and maturity, but a wall.

Konstantin Stanislavsky and his brother had this game they used to play — they would stand in a corner for five minutes and try not to think of . . . a white bear. The actors and audiences who were hamstrung at an early age by the Method had a similar problem. They got themselves in a corner and none of them ever succeeded in not thinking about themselves for five minutes.

The madness in the Method performed a frontal lobotomy on youth culture. The Method actors were not tortured — they merely should have been. ECT, I think.

By 1956, authority was an Aunt Sallie to be stoned outside

the city gates by any upwardly mobile malcontent with a ripe tomato. John Osborne was twenty-six at the start of that year, about the same age as the prototype Teds, and though hardly a dab hand with a bikechain Mr Osborne shared with them a kind of despairing patriotism (Britannia no longer ruled the Suez Canal, let alone the waves, and a lot of young men felt jilted), their stubborn pride and inbred inferiority feelings (the birthmarks of class) and a need to vent an abundant store of bitter bile accumulated over the years on some sitting ducks. But while the Teds were attacking Cypriots and West Indians, Osborne was laying into Sandhurst and the Royal Family.

Although nothing chooses safer targets for firing practice than wilful irreverence, when *Look Back in Anger* appeared at the Royal Court Theatre on 8 May 1956, the most popular theatrical vision of youthful hysterics was *Salad Days*. *Look Back in Anger* was the only red meat in town.

Though Osborne grew up to be Colonel Blimp with an Equity card, when it came to burning effigies of authority in 1956 there was no writer in the country who had a greater claim to lighting the pyre than he did. It is a telling measure of the social climate in which he grew up that he was expelled from the minor public school, Belmont College in Devon, in 1945 at the age of sixteen after badmouthing the Royal Family and slapping the face of Anthony Reynolds, the school's headmaster — not expelled for slapping the head *but for insulting the monarch*.

One year after *Look Back In Anger* Osborne wrote in *Declaration*, 'My objection to the Royal symbol is that it is dead, it is the gold filling in a mouthful of decay. While the cross symbol represents *values*, the crown simply represents a *substitute* for values. When the Roman crowds gather outside St Peter's, they are taking part in a moral *system*, however detestable it may be. When the mobs rush forward in the Mall they are taking part in the last circus of a civilization that has lost faith in itself, and sold itself for a splendid triviality, for the "beauty" of the ceremonial, and the "essential spirituality of the rite". We may not create any beauty or exercise much spirituality but by God! we've got the finest ceremonial and rites in the world! Even the Americans haven't got that.' It is reasonable to assume that ten years earlier Mr Osborne was couching the emotions of a Roundhead in briefer, more colourful terms.

Alan Carter, an Osborne biographer, said, 'Osborne achieved the initial breakthrough whilst Arden, Bolt, Delaney, Owen, Pinter, Wesker and others were waiting to carry the movement through. They had certain beliefs and attitudes in common, although their work is very different. Essentially they were left-wing, disillusioned and ir- reverent.'

In actual fact, what the Angries had in common was the fundamental reason for their anger. The Angries were angry about class – being lower-middle class, they didn't have any. It was class warfare – if a combination of career ambition and whingeing discontent can be termed warfare – camouflaged as a children's crusade, all grist for the cult of youth's relentless mill.

Jimmy Porter, the Angry Young Archetype himself, was the perfect blowpipe for Mr Osborne's poison arrows. 'Brother Nigel? The straight-backed chinless wonder from Sandhurst? The platitude from Outer Space – that's brother Nigel. He'll end up in the Cabinet one day, make no mistake.'

Kenneth Tynan, the *Observer*'s drama critic and *the* drama critic, swept aside the mixed reviews *Look Back in Anger* received (*The Times* and the *Daily Mirror* did not like it, while *The Sunday Times* and the *Daily Express* did) in a tidal wave of enthusiasm. 'All the qualities are there, qualities that one had despaired of ever seeing again on the stage – the drift towards anarchy, the instinctive leftishness, the automatic rejection of "official" attitudes, the surrealist sense of humour, the casual promiscuity, the sense of lacking a crusade worth fighting for, and underlying all these, the determination that no one who dies shall go unmourned. I agree that *Look Back in Anger* is likely to remain a minority taste. What matters, however, is the size of the minority. I estimate it at roughly 6,733,000, which is the number of people in this country between the ages of twenty and thirty. And this figure will doubtless be swelled by refugees from other age-groups who are curious to know precisely what the contemporary young pup is thinking and feeling. I doubt if I could love anyone who did not wish to see *Look Back in Anger*.'

This campaign for uncivil rights spilled over into a host of films demanding parity – *Room at the Top, A Kind of Loving* – wherein it was taken as read that the hero was licensed to whinge. In the kitchen sink dramas of the late Fifties and early Sixties, adapted from novels published a few years earlier, the hero is invariably 'trapped' by his girlfriend (she becomes pregnant and immediately turns into the old standby of the British cinema, the Frumpish Shrew). In short, the devil woman metamorphosed into *her mother* – who *never* liked the hero in the first place, and prevents him from – a precursor of the Me Generation, this – *fulfilling* himself, which in Kitchen Sinkspeak usually means listening to lowbrow classical music, the early Sixties equivalent of joining a squash club. The hero invariably rebels by coming back to hearth and home one night half cut and symbolically throwing up over the mother-in-law's Cyril Lord. Never before in the history of the cinema have audiences been expected to applaud a boy for bringing up his breakfast, but this was what the kitchen sink dramas demanded as their tawdry toll on credibility. In all probability this was how the British film industry died – not with a bang, but with a vomit.

The Beats were Bohemia where the buffalo roamed, old-style Bohemia transferred to postwar North America, lives of squalor and chaos, more time spent talking about art than doing it, but what was special about them was that they were American and they were mobile. Jack Kerouac's typewriter launched a million backpacks.

Jack Kerouac was a small town French-Canadian, a failed college football player, frustrated scribbler and loony – kicked out of the US Navy in 1943 for claiming to be Samuel Johnson (he was writing the unpublished *The Sea Is My Brother* at the time). Neal Cassady was a Mid-Western boy brought up in a series of unsalubrious hotels by his alcoholic dad. Between 1940 and 1944 Cassady stole five hundred cars in and around Denver. He was caught three times, and each time he was sent to reform school.

Neal Cassady had two interests in life – girls and cars. Jack Kerouac also had two interests in life – alcohol and

Neal Cassady.

Jack Kerouac wrote eighteen books about himself — he was incapable of having an ingrown toenail without being seized by a burning desire to tell the rest of the world about it — but he remained essentially a one hit wonder and, more importantly, a cipher. He had always soaked up and aped those around him — Allen Ginsberg, William Burroughs, Gary Snyder, Lucien Carr — but it was Cassady who made his life and work come alive.

On the Road was written between 1948 and 1956 and published in September 1957. A biographer of Mr Kerouac, Ann Charters, said, 'Kerouac's vision of Neal Cassady ('Dean Moriarty') in *On the Road* centred on one of the most vital fantasies of America, the dream of the cowboy, free and footloose, become a drifter with the crowding and commercialization of modern life. In the novel Jack's intuition made him visualize Neal as a cowboy standing naked in the New York apartment before they were introduced. *On the Road* caught a sense of the American folk-hero rebelliousness, the spirit of the wide, western plains in Cassady's colossal restlessness. Cassady was the loner in *On the Road*, the hero left with nothing at the end of the road. He was given epic proportions to live out Kerouac's visions, the sensual ecstatic joy of the road ("We know time, how to slow it up and walk and dig and just old-fashioned spade kicks, what other kicks are there?") and the vision of the despairing, senseless emptiness of the road. ("What's your road, man? – holyboy road, madman road, rainbow road, guppy road, any road. It's an any-where road for anybody anyhow. Where body how?")'

The reality of Kerouac's life — a middle-aged lush who lived with his mother until he died at the age of forty-seven — was overwhelmed by the dominant image of the work — roaming America, free as a bee. What *On the Road* promised was childhood with a driving licence. For many it was an offer they could not refuse and with their predilections for music, marijuana and mysticism the Beats were a hippie primer. The book made Kerouac famous though not rich — the largest advance he ever received was $7500. The *idea* of *On the Road* was infinitely more appealing than the reality of

31

the work — What I Did On My Holidays sold as a poetic idyll, a homo-erotic love story all the more tiresome for being platonic — though neither Jack nor Neal were strangers to biting their pillow — and inane prattlings dressed up as profundities — the book ends with the conclusion that 'God is Pooh Bear'. *Deep.*

If the success of the book was too much for its creator to cope with — gathering fat and despair like nuts in May in his mother's house — it was even tougher for *On the Road's* hero. Cassady was followed by the FBI soon after *On the Road's* publication, set up for a possession of marijuana rap (undercover agents gave him money to buy them dope and he blew it all at the racetrack but they nicked him anyway) and began serving a five-year sentence in San Quentin in May 1958. Sal Paradise and Dean Moriarty were never comfortable in each other's presence after that.

Kerouac was not a happy man. The Beats had two distinguishing features — extreme sexual generosity and mild radical rhetoric. Neither of these party pieces brought any joy to Saint Jack. 'My disciples think they're doing what I want them to do. They're fucking in front of me but all I can see is thighs.' It is unclear from this remark whether Kerouac wanted tighter sex standards or a better view. But he was just as unhappy on the barricades. Ann Charters says, 'He [Kerouac] had insisted he was apolitical in the old days, but as his friends [Allen Ginsberg, Gary Snyder, Philip Whalen] gained widespread recognition as radicals, he raged at them for not being, like him, American patriots.'

When Mr Ginsberg came out with lines like his considered political analysis on how to run the imminent American revolution — 'We'll go all the way out! We'll take our clothes off to read our poems!' — Kerouac reached for his vat of tokay. In the Sixties, Cassady became the driver of Ken Kesey's so-called Magic Bus, at the wheel once more, this time taking the LSD-addled so-called Merry Pranksters to destinations unknown. Kerouac was unsympathetic to hallucinogenics. After trying LSD once with Timothy Leary in 1961 — a bad experience, with Kerouac regressing to the time he was kicked out of the navy for being a fruitbat – Kerouac maintained that — heh heh — the Russians had introduced the drug into the country to weaken young Americans.

'*America it's them bad Russians,*' Allen Ginsberg had mocked, '*Them Russians them Russians and them Chinamen. And them Russians. The Russia wants to eat us alive. The Russia's power mad. She wants to take the cars from out our garages. Her wants to grab Chicago. Her needs a Red Readers Digest. Her wants our auto plants in Siberia. Him big bureauocracy running our filling stations. That no good. Ugh. Him make Indians learn read. Him need big black niggers. Hah. Her make us all work sixteen hours a day. Help.*'

But Kerouac was not taking that well-worn path to the Right that traditionally comes with advancing years, pickling brain and increasing wealth – he had been a follower of William Buckley for years. For three thousand dollars he wrote a syndicated article in 1969 in which he dismissed – and disowned – all of American counter-culture and the New Left. 'I'm pro-American,' he whimpered, 'and the radical political involvement seem to tend elsewhere . . . the country gave my Canadian family a good break, more or less, and we see no reason to demean said country.' When drunk, Kerouac would insist he was a US Marine and ready to go and fight in Vietnam at a moment's notice should Uncle Sam need him. He had come a long way since he concluded *On the Road* with, 'Don't you know that God is Pooh Bear?' Or perhaps he hadn't.

One of Jack Kerouac's abiding personal obsessioons – apart from his Neal – was a conviction that he was sterile. He insisted that he could not possibly be the father of his wife's child because he was incapable of reproduction. (*Jan Kerouac* – no relation!). But Jack Kerouac fathered a lifestyle, and a blood test to ascertain parentage was hardly necessary.

On the surface Mod appeared to be a mere reaction against the greasy yobbism of the Teds. But it went further and deeper than that. Mod represented the raised expectations of the most intelligent and metropolitan of working-class youth. Mod was the gap between full employment and unfulfilled aspirations, the missing link between bomb sites and Bacardi ads.

The earliest Mods were besotted with all thing conti-

nental – to them Modernism was a package tour of the
soul. Early Mod clubs in London were those that catered
primarily for a clientele of French students, Le Kilt and La
Poubelle. Proto-Mods wore Italian suits and French crops.
They suffered subtitled French films in silence. At least one
of them wondered aloud why Monsieur Marcel Marceau
never had any dialogue to speak. Mods became lapsed
Europeans when they decided they preferred the English
line in their suits and found they could not dance to Mireille
Mathieu.

Mods turned neatness into an art form. The phantom
totems of their style – an extra inch on the vents of their
jackets, the label of their shirt – meant they could be Mods
in the banks, insurance companies and shipping offices
where they worked. The demands on their time of these
same jobs meant that – despite Tiles, the noonday underground – the weekend was a time for Total Mod around
the clock. No cult before or since has placed such emphasis
on days off – Bank Holidays, the weekend. The calling card
of 'Ready, Steady Go!' – The Weekend Starts Here – was
more than just happenstance. Mod's mind's eye was
always calendar-watching.

Mod made its debut in *Town* magazine in 1962, with
interviews with and photographs of some young faces from
Stamford Hill. 'Bilgorri of Bishopsgate. He's a great tailor.
All the faces go to Bilgorri. And John Stephens. He's very
good on trousers.'

Young working-class males had never talked like this
before. Young Mark Feld, fifteen, who grew up to be young
Marc Bolan, told *Town* of some shirts in C&A. 'Some faces
won't look at them because they're only 14/6. That's just
ridiculous.' Warming to his theme, he recalled a gingham
shirt he had spied in Woolworth's that very morning. 'Only
ten bob. A few alterations and it would look as good as a
four guinea job from John Michael.'

The bespoke stylists who would serve the Mods so well
had served a long apprenticeship. Vince of Newburgh
Street had been selling flamboyant clothes to homosexuals
and showbusiness types since 1954. John Stephen had
worked there as an assistant and then struck out on his own
with £300 capital and a shop in Beak Street. After all the
stock was destroyed in a fire he started up again around the

corner where the rent was only £10 a week, and he invented Carnaby Street. Mod derived from Modernist, as in Modern jazz – it was sharp, clean, *modern*, everything they aspired to be. Charlie Mingus and Dave Brubeck, not Acker Bilk and Kenny Ball, Mod not Trad, dad. There were to be no goatee beards and sandals for these boys. Like the Teds, their music was American. Unlike the Teds, it was music made by American blacks. In *Generation X*, Hamblett and Deverson's Domesday Book of early Sixties' youth, a sixteen-year-old Mod says, 'At the moment we're hero-worshipping the spades – they can dance and sing . . . we do the Shake and the Hitch-Hiker to fast numbers but we're going back to dancing close because the spades do it.'

In 1962 some trailblazing Mods took up the traditional City Gent look – for a while a few of them even wore bowler hats and carried umbrellas. 'It didn't last long,' Johnny Moke said, 'but it's where the waisted suits came from.' From 1962 Mod suits were Anglo rather than Italian – a vote of confidence that would eventually lead to England Swinging and all that.

More casual clothes flowed into mainstream Mod, like the sportswear from Lonsdale in Beak Street (one Mod temple still extant). The Parka, worn for practical reasons by prototype Modernists, the scooter boys of 1959–60, evolved into part of Mod style as more faces got mobile.

It was frantic, fastidious, ever-changing stuff. One Mod who had been out of the country for a while said he dared not wear any of his suits until he discovered if the jacket's side vents should be five or six inches long. The amphetamine they consumed gave the Mods not only energy but also encouraged acute narcissism and bad complexions. Mods had it bad for themselves.

By now they were going to the Flamingo (called the Allnighter after the sun went down), the Scene and La Discotheque. The attraction of the Flamingo were the black American GIs who hung out there, from whom the Mods bought soul records unavailable in this country. Indigenous whiteys like the Beatles and the Stones, who coveted black American Mod favourites while still attempting to master the art of songwriting, were considered unspeakably non-U by the purists of facedom. The compulsive

35

consumerism of the Mods, so subtle that for a year or two it was submerged below the horizon of the grown-up world, finally got the treatment in 1963 when that august periodical *Hairdresser's Journal* told upwardly mobile barbers everywhere that, fee-fi-fo-fum, they smelled the cash of young Englishmen. 'Modernists, or Mods for short, account for about 35 per cent of Britain's male teenage population. Their fashions are the furthest out, the most up-to-the-second of any and the male Mod probably devotes between a quarter and a third of his weekly income to his appearance. As such, they represent a valuable clientele to the men's hairdresser who is prepared to give them the sleek, carefully-groomed styles they are looking for.'

Style was the Mod's antidote to the creeping paralysis of working-class life but, being working-class themselves, the Mods savoured a ritual outing to the seaside on a Bank Holiday as much as any old wrinklie in cloth cap and clogs. The early Mods abhorred violence − spending a small fortune on clothes each and every week is the greatest antidote to yobbism known to man − but the mass of newer, less cerebral Mods (and it *was* a mass movement by now − five 'Mod' magazines started in early 1964 and all sold between 250,000 to 500,000 copies per issue) were not so fastidious. Easter Sunday, 1964, at not-so-sunny Clacton was the coldest Easter day since 1884. There was little business for the shops and they closed early. A few local leather lads scuffled with visiting Mods. Some Easter eggs were pilfered by Mods with a sweet tooth. A few stones were thrown and a small pack of playful Mods went onto the pier without paying. Then everyone went home to Mum.

The next day every paper but *The Times* gave the modest exploits of the Mods in Clacton the front page. The *Daily Mirror*'s 'WILD ONES INVADE SEASIDE TOWN − SCOOTER GANGS BEAT UP CLACTON' was typical. The Home Secretary himself said, 'There was nothing like a riot or gang warfare. Clacton was not sacked.' But it would be − the reports were a self-fulfilling prophecy and on the next Bank Holiday Clacton, along with Margate, Hastings, Bournemouth, all played host to real riots.

Dr George Simpson, a Margate magistrate, held a special session of his court on Whit Monday to hear the cases of the forty-four youths who had been charged. Sentencing a Mod to three months in prison, Dr Simpson said, 'It is not likely that the air of this town had ever been polluted by the hordes of hooligans, male and female, such as we have seen this weekend and of whom you are an example. These long-haired, mentally unstable, petty little hoodlums, these sawdust Caesars who can only find courage like rats, in hunting in packs, came to Margate with the avowed intent of interfering with the life and prosperity of its inhabitants. Insofar as the law gives us power, this court will not fail to use the prescribed penalties. It will, perhaps, discourage you and others of your kidney who are infected with this vicious virus.'

Cute Lord Arran, writing in the *Evening News*, was more pragmatic about the riots. 'I am truly sorry for Clacton — a nice, warm-hearted place. If some town had to cop it, I would have preferred Frinton. They are snooty in Frinton.'

The Rockers were few in number and IQ, beer, bird and bike-orientated. These motorway Neanderthals were not so much a subculture, more a part of the Great British Hooligan tradition. Although forever linked in the media's mind with Mods, the acrimonious bond did not run too deep; for a start Mods were urban creatures and Rockers were throwbacks of the countryside — they did not see much of each other except on special occasions, like Easter. They were part-time mutual punchbags and tormentors, nothing more. Mods spent very little time thinking about Rockers, or indeed about anything other than themselves.

Swinging London was what happened when late Mod brushed up against early Hippie — the effect on Mod could be diagnosed as fatal, but a closer examination shows that it was not the Sixties that killed Modernism. There was a purity about Mod that all other cults have lacked. There was no toy angst in Modernism and no 'stars', 'celebrities' or 'personalities' to satisfy the crawling conceit of show-business. They did not compete, except with each other. Mod produced no one that the grown-ups could pat on the head and come to call their own, no one to flatter and corral (the Who were a clever, clumsy travesty). The only hoops that Mods jumped through were of their own making.

Mod was not finally killed by the taint of Hippie, commercial assimilation or bad press. It died out because none of the heroic foot soldiers of Modernism would see seventeen again. In the Eighties, economic hard times stunt a young man's growth, making it possible for him to run with a cultural pack well into his twenties. Back when the world was still Modern, young people grew up faster.

Hippie was what happened to Bohemia when it had access to unprecedented amounts of money and drugs. These young people had never had it so good – no one had – and that was why they wanted to change society. They could afford to take the time out to do it. What money and drugs did to Bohemia was to get it off its butt. In some cases it got it off its butt and onto its feet. In others it got it off its butt and onto its back.

In the mainstream of Hippie there were always two currents – the Personal ('After the Doors, it just wasn't the same sitting down to dinner with your parents') and the Political ('Be the first one on your block to have your boy come home in a box'). Ironies abounded – the Personal wing of Hippie, with its stress on the dubious liberating qualities of chemical excess and limitless sexual generosity was not so intimate that it did not harbour dreams of ruling the world, while the fact that the Political wing of Hippie put real pressure on the US Government to pull out of Vietnam and paid the price in blood that did not taste of tomatoes has to be evaluated in the atmosphere of the times – lethargy and pacifism hung so heavy in the hedonistic air of the late Sixties that it is highly likely that almost as many draft cards would have been burned if the US Army had been fighting Nazi Germany rather than its diametrical opposite the Viet Cong – the most saintly army that ever lived and killed.

'The violence in Vietnam is not seen in isolation,' Richard Neville wrote. 'It is related to the violence inherent in corporate bureaucracy, the unconscious violence of the conveyor belt.' Statistics for the proportion of factory workers napalmed in their staff canteens by the US Air Force during the 1960s are unavailable.

The misspent idealism of the Hippies was overshadowed and purified by the psychotic sentimentality of their opponents. 'If you decide to burn your draft card,' croaked Victor Lundberg in 'An Open Letter To My Teenage Son', 'then burn your birth certificate at the same time. From that moment I have no son.'

History does not record whether or not Lundberg Junior heeded Dad's advice, but by the time of this masterpiece of maudlin emotional blackmail − 'An Open Letter To My Teenage Son' entered the US charts on 25 November 1967, reached number ten and dropped out after three weeks − the burning of draft cards (or Selective Service System cards, to give them the name the US Government knew them by) was a wild fire, out of control and impossible to put out.

Only two years before, twenty-two-year-old David Miller had been arrested by the FBI and became the first man to be charged with violating a law passed a few months earlier by President LBJ preventing the destruction of draft cards. Mr Johnson's press secretary informed the media that, 'David Miller is giving our adversaries a false picture of what the people in this country actually feel.' He was about as wrong as it was possible to be.

The nature of the war America fought against Vietnam allowed conscientious objectors to feel more righteous than any conscientious objector has ever felt, before or since. The nature of Selective Service only added to that sense of righteousness.

David Pichaske said in *A Generation in Motion*, 'Selective Service, the way it drafted the poor and the black and sent them off to die, while waving the white sons of middle-class Americans safely by into college and 2-S deferments, and the way the 2-S hung over your head once you got into school − burn your draft card and you lose it, thumb your nose at the Dean and get expelled from school and you lose it: and then it's straight to boot camp and straight to San Diego and straight to Nam and home in a wooden box. So they really *had* you, and it *was* all connected, just as you had always suspected.'

American Hippie had its roots in Beat and British Hippie grew out of Swinging London − that point in time when

Mod wafted off into the firmament in a cloud of marijuana smoke and Lord Snowdon caused a sensation by wearing a white polo-neck. But soon the evolved Beats learned to swing and the evolved swingers came to smell – they were forged into one long-haired homogenous international conspiracy and flourished with rock music as their universal fertilizer. Thanks to delusions of profundity inspired by Bob Dylan's pitifully obscure lyrics and the irony-numbing effect of mind-contraction drugs like LSD and marijuana, rock music had traded its purity, vulgarity and *joie de teen* for the alleged 'raising of consciousness' and an inverted, pitiable respectability.

For all of Hippie's supposed political conscience, while the blacks were burning Watts most whites were burning joss sticks. Hallucinogenic honkies consumed LSD with the religious fervour of a penitent fondling his rosary – for the very first time, pop was a vehicle for disgusting religious appetites. Even those fun-fun-funsters the Beach Boys had a Maharishi. Ringo Beatle may have returned from India complaining that it was 'just like Butlins' but – like the past and the sub-continent that was spawning a plethora of gurus-to-the-stars – sanity was another country. Brian Epstein was being buried, unmourned by the boys he had loved and made impossible not to love. Highbrow critics raised on the classics, fans of Sibelius rather than Sam the Sham, swooned like bobbysoxers over *Sergeant Pepper's Lonely Hearts Club Band*, pop music's Pearl Harbor.

Abbie Hoffman wrote in the introduction to *Steal This Book* about the Yippie blueprint for a new society (Mr Hoffman cutely defined a Yippie as a Hippie who had been hit on the head by a policeman) – '*Steal This Book* is, in a way, a manual of survival in the prison that is America. It preaches jailbreak. It shows you where and exactly how to place the dynamite that will destroy the walls. The first section – SURVIVE! – lays out a potential action program for our new Nation. The chapter headings spell out the demands for a free society. A community where the technology produces goods and services for whoever needs them, come who may. It calls on the Robin Hoods of Santa Barbara Forest to steal from the Robber Barons who own the castle of capitalism. It implies that the reader is already "Ideologically Set", in that he understands corporate feudalism as the only robber worthy of being called "crime", for it is committed against the people as a whole. Whether the ways it describes to rip-off shit are legal or illegal is irrelevant. The dictionary of law is written by the bosses of order. Our moral dictionary says no to heisting from each other. To steal from a brother or sister is evil. To *not* steal from the institutions that are the pillars of the Pig Empire is equally immoral.'

The rhetoric was showing a lot of rot. By the Summer of Love − Hippie's great recruitment drive − some of Hippie's founding fathers had discovered that the pie in the tangerine sky was inedible and turned away, disillusioned. The Diggers were the soup kitchens of West Coast psychedelia, handing out free nosh to hungry heads. In 1967, a former Digger reflected sourly on the end of free food; 'Well, man, it took a lot of organization to get that done. We had to scuffle to get the food. Then the chicks or somebody[!] had to prepare it. Then we got to serve it. A lot of people got to do a lot of things at the right time or it doesn't come off. Well, it got so that people weren't doing it. I mean a cat wouldn't let us have his truck when we needed it or some chick is grooving somewhere else and can't help out. Now you hate to get into a power bag and start telling people what to do, but without that, man, well.'

The reason for the crusading inertia of the Hippies was not so much that they took drugs but that the drugs they took were all guaranteed to render the user happy as a sandboy in a state of torpid euphoria. 'So much dope was given away to friends, free,' David Pichaske recalled dreamily. 'Because you wanted to open for them the worlds that had been opened for you and it was *so beautiful* to watch them when the dream came.' Creepy!

Hippie failed to affect the real world because it had found so many wondrous, internal worlds to wander through. But while the Hippies eschewed reality, the real world was discovering the commercial properties of Hippie. *Hair* opened on 17 October 1967 in the Astor Library in Greenwich Village before moving on to the Cheetah discotheque, then to the Biltmore on Broadway, then to the world. The

41

soundtrack album sold more than five million copies. *Rolling Stone* sniffed haughtily that the music in *Hair* was no more rock than that of the music of a toothpaste commercial.

Others turned on to Hippie not for commercial reasons but for the credibility it would bring. The dear departed Monkees made a film in 1968 called *Head*, which lost them the love of the children who were their adoring constituency while failing to ingratiate them with the Hippies whose approval they coveted. Hippie was a closed shop.

The Yippies' New Deal swiftly degenerated into petty crime and endless cant. 'In New York, 1968,' Richard Neville said, 'I was present at a Yippie meeting in Union Park in which a department store loot-in was being planned. 'We'll choose a shop. About twenty of us will go in, select the stuff we want, hand the cashier a flower and head towards the door.'

But man cannot live by floral arrangements alone. The delusions of self-sufficiency harboured by the Hippies persisted beyond the point in their history when it became clear that the very existence of the Hippies was totally dependent on hand-outs from the straight world — Woodstock. Although popular myth has long perceived Woodstock as the ultimate fulfilment of Hippie ideals and Altamont as the death of the dream, in reality it was Woodstock that most perfectly spotlighted the hypocrisies, helplessness and hapless lethargy of the Hippies.

Woodstock! That wonderful love nation you'll remember for ever! See the movie, buy the triple album!

Car-owning Hippies clogged up the highway to Woodstock in an eight-mile traffic jam, while a thunderstorm falling out of the August sky turned the site into a muddy bog. The police declared Woodstock 'a disaster area', and they were not wrong. The only sustenance available on the site was a chemical co-op selling copious supplies of opium, LSD, psilocybin, mescaline, marijuana and hashish. In their rush to the promised swampland it had never occurred to the Hippies that their stomachs would not be kept as full as the family freezer. There was nothing to drink and no food in the land of plenty. Counterculture capitalists twenty-four-year-old investment broker John Roberts and twenty-five-year-old entrepreneur Mike Lang, the big daddies behind Woodstock, had been too busy rushing in the cameras and recording equipment to set up a single hot dog stand.

Soon the half a million jolly campers of Woodstock were starving – but help was at hand for the ravenous ravers. The local Women's Group of the Jewish Community Centre spoonfed the frontiersmen of Utopia 30,000 sandwiches. Woodstock's owner, middle-aged dairy farmer Mr Max Yasgur, donated huge quantities of milk and cheese to prevent the gurgling inmates of his farm from wasting away. Even the originally outraged residents of Woodstock warmed to the plight of the helpless Hippie nation when the prospect of turning a fast buck out of the dawning of the Age of Aquarius beckoned.

But most of all the Hippies had President Nixon's Armed Forces to thank for helping them to stave off the pangs of hunger. Instead of saying 'Let them eat love beads' as might have been expected after all those charred draft cards, the Air Force was sent in with a small mountain of edible treats. Despite all the protests about the bombs, napalm and Agent Orange that the same Air Force was dropping on the Vietnamese, the peanut butter sure tasted swell. Manna from heaven, courtesy of President Richard M. Nixon.

When the playpen was dismantled at the end of the three-day fling – on the other side of the country, Sharon Tate had been dead for seven days, murdered by some longhairs from way back – the head of Monticello's constabulary was full of praise: 'Notwithstanding their personality, their dress and their ideas, they are the most courteous, considerate and well-behaved group of kids I have ever been in contact with in my twenty-four years of police work.'

The praise of the police for the Hippies was echoed by the Hippies' praise of the Hippies – Woodstock was perceived by them as the stuff that the Birth Of A Nation is made of. *Any movement that celebrated an event like Woodstock as some kind of moral triumph made an event like Altamont inevitable.*

Despite attacking antiwar demonstrators with the ferocity of National Guardsmen the Hell's Angels, those rancid reactionaries on sparkling Harleys, had been elevated to folk hero status by such counterculture luminaries as acid-testing dilettante Ken 'Cuckoo Nest' Kesey and marathon rockers the Grateful Dead. All the nice heads loved a biker.

It was the Grateful Dead's leader, Jerry Garcia, who provided glowing references for the Hell's Angels when the Rolling Stones, at the height of an American tour, decided to play a massive free festival and desired exotic bouncers. The Rolling Stones' desire to play such a festival was brought on by chance — the first they had ever had to grab the role of ultimate rock heroes, a post that had become vacant with the Beatles in the throes of a painful divorce and Bob Dylan absent from the scene playing the role of hermit family man.

But the Rolling Stones did not want any establishment pigs at the Californian speedway track of Altamont, just outside San Francisco — they would provide their own alternative police force. It was fitting that they, with all their tiresome celebratory dabblings in Satanism, voyeuristic violence, dirty hypodermic needles and other habits which were the direct antithesis of love, peace, tolerance and good vibes, should choose to replace one crew of law enforcers with another of far greater brutality. The doublethink was ripe for its nemesis.

In the last month of the last year of the Sixties, 300,000 people hooked down the depression cocktail of tranquillizers and cheap wine, fending off the freezing December air as they huddled on the bleak hills around the Altamont speedway by setting fire to mountains of garbage. The Hell's Angels, who had been paid five hundred dollars' worth of beer to keep the peace and love intact, were already brutalizing the audience by the time the first act of the festival — admittedly Santana, bad enough to put anybody in a vicious mood — were on stage. In front of the stage a boy was repeatedly kicked in the face by a Hell's Angel and the set was — some would say mercifully — interrupted by another ugly Angel rushing across the stage on his way to beat up someone else.

When Jefferson Airplane played their guitarist Marty Balin was knocked senseless (even more senseless, rather) by a pool cue-wielding Angel for having the audacity to intervene in one of the many beatings being handed out by the bikers. Ludicrously, trembling with fear and with their lead guitarist unconscious, Jefferson Airplane launched into their rebel-rousing anthem, 'Up Against The Wall, Motherfucker'. In complete control by now, the Angels drove their machines through the packed crowd to park them by the side of the stage. At the end of a set by Crosby, Stills, Nash and Young, a horde of stretcher bearers were sent out into the audience and came back with their cargo of bloody, unconscious humans on their way to the First Aid tent.

After a lengthy delay it was time for the Darlings of Darkness themselves. The Rolling Stones appeared and found themselves confined to a dinky stage area sur-rounded by jeering, openly contemptuous Hell's Angels who found a source of great mirth in Mick Jagger's fruity dancing. As they swaggered into the appalling 'Sympathy For The Devil' a group of Hell's Angels some ten yards from the stage stabbed and kicked to death a young black man, one Meredith Hunter, who had offended the sensitive nature of the Angels by attending the festival with his girlfriend who was very pretty and very white.

'The violence seemed just another stage setting for the Stones routine,' wrote Sol Stern. 'They continued to play, mostly uninterrupted, while the fights flared again and again across the front of the stage.'

They made a movie of it, of course, in which Mick Jagger wept as he watched a slow motion replay of the murder of Meredith Hunter – a white singer who owed everything he had to the inspiration of black musicians watching the killing of a black man by white men as the white crowd looked on with passive resignation. Mr Keith Richard demonstrated considerably less compassion, or was per-haps less conscious of the camera; 'People were just asking for it. All those nude, fat people had victims' faces.'

'Altamont', wrote Greil Marcus, 'did not in and of itself "end" anything. Rather, as Robert Christgau has said, it provided an extraordinarily complex and visceral metaphor for the *way* things of the Sixties ended. All the symbols were marshalled, and the crowd turned out, less to have a good time than to help make counterculture history. The result was that the counterculture, in the form of rock and roll, Hell's Angels ("Our outlaw brothers," as many liked to call them), and thousands of politicized and unaffiliated young people, turned back upon itself. No one knew how to deal with a spectacle that from the moment it began contradicted every assumption on which it had been based, producing violence instead of fraternity, selfishness instead of generosity, ugliness instead of beauty, a bad trip instead of a high.'

As the Hippies were discovering the hollowness of their aspirations and promises, big business had more disposable income than first impressions may have led one to believe. The wonder of Hippie had filtered through to the Man himself. Hollywood waited until the end of the Sixties before discovering the decade, although films like *The Activist* (1969), *The Strawberry Statement* (1970) and *RPM* (1970) had less to do with what Hippie meant than what the box office boom enjoyed by the low budget *Easy Rider* meant — namely, where there's heads, there's bread.

At the same time a magazine advertisement featured a photograph of the masses squatting in the fields of Farmer Yasgur with the respectful caption, 'Woodstock Music Festival, 1969'. Under the golden memory was the legend IF THERE'S ONE THING ANVIL UNDERSTANDS, IT'S WHAT YOU WEAR, followed by an ingratiating hard sell spiel: 'We don't pretend to understand everything that's going on in your world today. But there is one thing we do know. We make slacks and jeans that a lot of guys go for. For a lot of good reasons. Like the way they fit. The way they'll stand up through any occasion. The fabrics they come in, made with Celanese Fortrel. And how little they sell for, starting at seven dollars.

'Granted, we're not hip to everything that's happening today, but what we are hip to, you might like. Our company may be seventy-two years old, but our slacks and jeans are definitely for the under thirties.'

Even *Playboy* had decided that love and peace were blood relatives of Mr Hugh Hefner's swinging pseudo-philosophy. The cover of the September 1970 issue featured a headband-wearing, peace sign-flashing 'hippie chick', the shadow of her peace sign forming the silhouette of the Bunny sign – nudge-nudge, man. Although Hippie dragged on well into the Seventies, this then was what all the cosmic aspirations had degenerated into – a marketing device. Entertainment for men.

Like El Cid's corpse propped up on his horse to frighten the Moors, a youth cult is artificially kept alive by its lowest ranks when the roots of the thing are withered and dead. The lowest ranks who perform this function are not the most devoted of the cult's participants, merely the most stupid.

Stan Cohen said, 'The more extravagant Mods who were involved in the whole rhythm and blues, camp, Carnaby Street scene were merging into the fashion-conscious Hippies (sic) and the incipient Underground, while the 'hard Mods' (wearing heavy boots, jeans with braces, short hair . . . jumpy . . . on the paranoiac edge) began to turn away from the fancy arabesques of acid rock to champion ska, rock steady and reggae.' When Mod died, the desire of a large number of working-class youths to be what they thought of as clean and hard – as opposed to dirty and soft, a.k.a. Hippie – did not abate, even after they had long stopped thinking of themselves as Mods, hard or otherwise. Not all young people had foliage in their hair and bells on their toes in the Sixties. Certainly not those who could be seen on the football terraces on a Saturday afternoon and mooching around under the plastic palm trees some hours later.

Skinheads appeared in the late Sixties and they were a product of that decade just as surely as the flower persons were. Skinheads' appearance was a loving, lame-brained parody of working-class (unskilled) manhood. They had a sense of community, a working-class urban community that no longer existed, if it ever had. The East End was a kind of Camelot, a lost Avalon, to many Skinheads. Out in the Home Counties, in the New Towns, Skinhead was massive.

Like Jay Gatsby – and every other youth cult – the Skinheads invented themselves. 'Whereas the Mods explored the upwardly mobile option,' Phil Cohen wrote, 'the Skinheads explored the lumpen.'

The first Skinheads felt excluded from all aspects of revelant youth culture yet this very exclusion was the basis of their sense of identity, the first step to creating their own defined, defensive community. The Skinheads put great emphasis on the defense of territory, helping one's mates in tight corners, all the trappings of hysterical masculinity at bay. The Kray brothers were prototype Skinheads. The Hippies had attempted to erode traditional standards of masculinity, and the Skinheads wanted revenge. 'Hippie-bashing' — as well as 'Paki-bashing' and 'Queer-bashing' — was reputed to be a favoured leisure activity of the Skinheads, though most of the blood spilled by Skinheads originally flowed in the veins of other Skinheads. Because they were afraid of almost everything, Skinheads felt impelled to act as if they were afraid of nothing.

'I'll tell you why I hate the bloody Paks,' said one member of the Skinhead Brains Trust. 'I'll tell you a story. A week or so ago I was walking down the street with a couple of mates. I wanted a light for my fag. So I walked up to this Paki git and ask him, "You got a light, mate?" and what do you think the fucker did? I'll tell you. He walks — no, *runs* — into this shop and buys me a box of matches! Now, I ask you! What the fuck could I do with a bleeder like that but hit him? And another thing. Have you ever been in their restaurants? Have you seen the way they grovel round you, the way they're always trying to please you? I hate them, that's all.' *Rolling Stone*, the dope-smoker's *Reader's Digest*, surveying the scene in Merry Olde England in their issue of July 1969, were filled in on the subject of hippie-bashing by a skinhead who professed nothing but ennui for the pastime. 'Weirdos is no fun to jump though, because they don't fight back. They just curl up when you kick them.'

The declaration was a cover for the fact that Skinheads loved nothing better than a soft target. They were cowards the way only bullies can be cowards, hunting in packs, always ready to attack if they caught a whiff of fear. That West Indians were not a popular Skinhead target had nothing to do with the Skinhead party line that 'the blacks are more like us' than the Asians, and even less to do with the Skinheads' acquired taste (another reaction against the white whimsy of Hippie) for rock steady, bluebeat, ska and reggae. Blacks were left alone because Skinheads discovered that they fought back.

But they still seconded the motion submitted by the Teds fifteen years earlier that, as a member of a youth tribe, it is entirely possible to love black music and hate blacks.

In 1976 times were still easy enough to kick up a fuss. The year marked the last exit to bedlam.

Punk was a declaration of UDI.

It was a rebellion *not* against the world, but against the music business and what it had become. The Punk credo – Do It Yourself! – meant that almost all of the early Punk acolytes had a personal career stake in Punk's success. Of the few dozen people who went down into the mirrored subterranean depths of the Roxy in late 1976, almost all of them were musicians, writers, photographers or designers. The No Future generation all knew *exactly* what they wanted to do when they grew up. The musicians, writers, photographers and designers they wished to replace were for the most part so irredeemably dull that their cause was given a righteousness that was inflamed by amphetamine sulphate into a zeal that could pass for revolutionary.

Although the Punks claimed to despise everything that had gone before – *'No Elvis, Beatles or the Rolling Stones . . . in 1977'* foresaw the Clash, the Madam Rosas of the movement – with their basic bass-drums-guitar line-up and their songs of righteous indignation, the Punk bands were traditionalists, very much rock and roll's last stand. Punk's major achievement was the abolition of the flared trouser – the most noble abolition since William Wilberforce outlawed this country's slave trade.

In Punkese, 'Hippie' was a greater term of abuse than 'baby-molester' or 'mother-eater'. The Hippie were hairy, middle-class and peaceable – Punks were tufty-topped, working-class and aggressive, or so they claimed. One thing that the Punks really hated about the Hippies was that, even in 1976, the Hippies were still entrenched in a lot of the positions *that the Punks wanted for themselves.* The Hippies were taking up too much *space.* Bloody Hippies, coming over here, taking our jobs . . .

Another thing that the Punks hated about the heads, though they never said, was that they reminded them of themselves. Punks and Hippies were a lot more alike than either sect cared to admit. There was much dope-smoking on both sides. Where the Hippies had looked to the Far East for a 'better way', so many Punks also had a sort of spiritual homeland, getting all dewy-eyed when they thought of Jamaica. The very worst thing about attending any kind of Punk event in 1976—78 was the interminable number of reggae records that would be played before anything remotely listenable happened onstage (and invariably the five-chord thrash that would come from the stage would be, at best, remotely listenable). Punk's fascination for Jamaica is where Boy George O'Dowd, an ex-Punk himself, gleaned the inspiration for his original ridiculous hairdo.

Punk also had a social conscience that was embarrassingly like that of the Hippies — Punks, like the freaks they professed to despise, were all radical style and no content. The bottom dropped out of the idealistic passion market for a number of reasons. Marching in demos took a lot of energy and Punks, being the delicate little flowers that all night owls are, preferred to conserve their energy for when the sun went down. And Punks found that they did not much care for the lifetime radicals of the Socialist Workers Party, the dogma walkers behind such noble pressure groups as Rock Against Racism and the Anti-Nazi League. SWP people were Not Quite Our Type. They knew nothing about the Punk sense of theatre, of melodrama, they did not understand that Punks — for all their Karl Marx T-shirts and talk of 'anarchy' — were essentially showbiz kids: as lazy and liberal as *that*. Many Punks ceased to be politically concerned when they moved out of their squat, found a place to call their own and rented their first remote control TV set.

But the early Punks, the ravenous ones, had a sense of drama that no outsider could comprehend. Being a Punk meant never having to say please and thank you. Most of them were sweet, well-spoken working-class children, but they played the part of barbarians at the gates of the record industry because that was what was expected of them. It was their meal ticket. Things *had* got unbelievably stale and dull and Punk rhetoric – talk of killing Hippies and being into chaos not music – was used to emphasize the points they were making and trying to score. Punks had been feverish fans of David Bowie, the New York Dolls, Roxy Music, T. Rex and Gary Glitter – the importance of props and costume, bikechains and swastika armbands, was in their blood. 'I felt unclean for about forty-eight hours,' boasted a GLC councillor after witnessing a Sex Pistols concert – a rave review.

Punk was a marvellous career opportunity for a sizeable number of disaffected youth on the fringes of show-business. Things really had sunk as low on the pop front as the Punks accused; they promised to liven things up and they did. Soon Punk – a prototype YOP scheme – was giving all these disaffected young people a chance to spout off on any subject that came into their heads, and people listened. Most of what the Punks (especially myself) came out with was over-excited, half-baked drivel that would have been better confined to an undergraduate midnight oil bull session yet, by its very gregarious nature, Punk required it be produced for public consumption. Being involved in Punk was what some lucky people did instead of going to university – giant corporations like CBS and IPC generously providing the grants.

The early Punks talked a lot about bridging the gap between entertainers and audiences, a backlash against the huge stadium concerts, so much in vogue in the mid-Seventies, where a hundred thousand suckers would pay good money to see four or five ants cavorting half a mile away. But the gap the Punks talked of bridging was not merely physical, they were not just talking about a return to sweaty little dives – Punks purported to be men of the People and they would not, they said, become alienated from their everloving audience the way that glamorous grandfathers like the Stones and the Who had. But this was easy to say when playing the Roxy to a few dozen chums and associates – creative people! *Like oneself!* – and harder to sustain when Punk broke out to a mass audience, which it did very quickly thanks mostly to all the shock-horror front page tabloid headines grabbed by the

Sex Pistols saga.

A lot of young people, younger than the founding fathers of Punk, had heard about Punk and liked what they heard. Yes, things were dull. Yes, we hear what you're saying! Yes, WE WANT ACTION! Where do we get tickets?

Soon the Punk bands were playing venues that only a few months earlier they had sworn they would never pass the portals of – the Hammersmith Odeon, scene of many an old Hippie rave-up, became a popular Punk stamping ground, as did the Finsbury Park Rainbow, North London's little Woodstock itself. There were a lot of people who wanted to see Punk in all its rancid glory and there was a lot more money to be made than could ever be collected down the Roxy (where the regular clientele was all on the guest list anyway).

But it was not picking up the large box office takings that threw Punk into a deep depression from which it would never recover. What hurt was all these . . . *punks*, they called themselves, the kids in their imitation Sex shop duds who were turning up at the Rainbow and the Hammersmith Odeon to watch the Clash or the Jam – they were *awful!* In its early days Punk had been like a gentleman's club, a kind of Bloomsbury Set in bondage trousers. Now all these . . . *punks* had arrived on the scene and the way some of them behaved was just *too* much! They *spat* at the band when it was onstage, they jumped up and down in a frantic Pogo dance just like they had read they were expected to in the *Sun*, they made a big deal about doing a line of sulphate – worse still, some of them didn't take drugs at all. And if the support act was some worthy band of black brothers, some real Trenchtown rockers, these . . . *punks* were highly likely to jeer and pelt them with empty lager cans until they retired hurt. Very embarrassing, very distressing.

By 1977 – only one year after 'Anarchy in the UK' – the media had tamed the savage beast and came to treat it like a music hall turn, a novelty. The *News of the World* and the *Sunday People* ran articles on Punk babies, Punk-Ted weddings, all kinds of Punk cuteness while *Woman's Own* did a feature on daughters who were Punks too entitled 'Punks and Mothers'. Creepy!

But it was this gap between the Punk acolytes and their audience that cut deepest. A German general in the First World War said the British Army were, 'Lions led by donkeys'; with Punk, the reverse was so. As Puff the Magic Dragon finally called it quits and sadly slipped back into his cave, so the first Punks gradually deserted their sinking movement and got on with their careers. Ring the bell, Jack, the No Future Generation was on the bus.

Leaderless, the Punks fragmented into a passion for every cult that had ever walked the face of the King's Road — soon there were Skinheads, Punks, Teddy Boys and — *après* the 2-Tone storm in a teacup — Toy Mods on every street corner. But nothing new — the cult of teenage was derelict now, like the country house of impoverished gentry, open to coach trip plebs to tramp through for a shilling, asked to contibute nothing but their entrance fee.

Half-hearted attempts to stem the tide of jerry-built revivalism were shoddy in the extreme — the New Romantics of the early Eighties and the Casuals of a few years later built their house on nothing but nerky clothes and, in the case of the Romantics (who were all a good two stone too heavy ever to look exquisite or elegant; it would have been easier to feel romantic about a waste disposal unit) even nerkier music. The New Romantics' contribution to humanity was boys in frocks, hardly a cause for street parties and celebration. All the Casuals did was push up the price of sportswear to ridiculous heights and make it fashionable to wear silly-patterned cardigans that would not have looked out of place moping in Val Doonican's wardrobe.

In 1984 Levis were considering reintroducing the flared trouser. Things had sunk so low that they might find a market. Angry Young Attitudes were a thing of the past. Along with bad skin and self-pity, teenagers now came equipped with a white flag. The Eighties are the Dark Ages of teenage rebellion.

These days it is no longer formalized, savoured, celebrated. It exists only in likeable travesties such as 'Bad Boys' by Wham! (the happiest boys in showbusiness; says George Michael of success, 'It's a dream. I regularly sit back and think, God! I can't believe what I'm doing. I can't believe that I can do what I want at my age. This has got to be one of the only businesses in the world where you have as much money as you need, you feel secure, and you have no one to answer to. It's absolutely brilliant! What better job could you have than that?'), George and Andrew's angriest moment, wherein our twenty-year-old heroes, their maturity stunted by Monetarism/World Wide Recession (you pay your party dues and you take your choice) and the economic necessity of many young people of living with the old folks well into the outer suburbs of youth and practically into their own wrinkled dotage, tell their parents – in no uncertain terms! – that they can't tell the Bad Boys what time to get in that night because, in the words of the song, *I'm big enough to kick down the door!'* And in fleeting moments of Outside Broadcast Unit *cinéma verité* on the 'Nine O'Clock News', the ancient rites of hooliganism, as things are thrown at policemen hiding behind transparent riot shields from the streets of Toxteth or the terraces of Stamford Bridge.

And no one ever whitened Mother's hair, no one was ever nominated for an Academy Award for *that*.

Never again will teenagers waltz around the American-speaking world as if they owned the place.

Which they did.

Are You Sitting Comfortably?

Being a child is horrible. It is slightly better than being a tree or a piece of heavy machinery but not half as good as being a domestic cat. You share all the vulnerability and risk of ill-treatment while enjoying none of the freedom; if you should manage to evade being mauled by your drooling, drab, sour-smelling male parent, you are still going to be rubbished and generally interfered with, of that you may be sure.

Take your culture. It will have been created by adults of a perverted or at best whimsical mien. Intelligent people are simply not drawn towards the creation of children's culture. Your books will be full of talking animals and smiling mothers, i.e. they will be a pack of lies, peopled by mythical beasts masquerading as regular guys. Or worse still, if you live in the NW1 postal district of London you will read books that *are* realistic, not to mention utterly depressing; *Sophie's Mummy is a Fag Hag, Brian Was Hatched in a Test Tube, Yasmin Has a Clitorectomy*. In 1984 the unshockable Samaritans − those early pioneers of telephone sex − were shocked to find children as young as eight threatening suicide; five'll get you ten that it was the rising tide of gritty, socially relevant children's literature that pushed the tearful tinies over the edge.

But there has always been a dark, savage side to children's culture; it has always veered crazily, schizophrenically between the saccharine and the strychnine. From the nineteenth-century collections of folk tales by Hans Christian Andersen and Jacob and Wilhelm Grimm to the cautionary tales of the Victorians, there has always been an adult obsession with children being fattened up for slaughter, being eaten by beasts, being burned to a crisp. Just why this is, whether from a good impulse – a desire to warn the child that the world is often a dangerous place – or a bad one – simply to screw the child up, a notorious source of exquisite pleasure to more solid citizens than anyone cares/dares to admit – is unclear; but it is a fact that adults, with the supreme stupidity they are famous for, stuff children to bursting point with Grimm's reapers through all of their formative years and then turn round and bleat 'Oh, children are so *cruel!*'

TV is *the* children's medium; on tap, requiring no mobility or skills, the vacant, ever-available babysitter. As if to fight fears that television would coarsen and cheapen captive humanity, particularly the smaller sort, the earliest children's TV was impossibly genteel and vapid. Try serving up the sort of swill that the BBC, under the disgustingly bovine heading *Watch With Mother*, served up from the smug, stupid Fifties until well past the Profumo Affair to the tinies of today, and you would have major riots on your hands. The be-strung stable of stiff-jointed stars were all unbelievably meek, mild and mediocre – there was Andy Pandy, an effete prancing boy doll plastered in rouge and swathed in satin rompers – a great male role model. The most decisive, dynamic thing Andy Pandy ever did was raise a wooden hand and wave goodbye after the allotted ten minutes of torture by boredom. There was Muffin the Mule, an inane, capering quadruped who danced gracelessly on a piano played by his chair-bound cheerleader, an unfortunate Joyce Grenfell impersonator who trilled a never-changing song of rhetorical revelry and self-celebration: *'Who wants Muffin?/ Muffin the Mule!/ Dear old Muffin/ Playing the fool!'* The mothers of Great Britain were always mindful to keep the smelling salts at hand during Muffin's performances, least their little charges should be moved to swoon with sheer animal excitement.

There were Pinky and Perky, two highly unlikely pigs, who were also recording stars – and not half bad, when you weren't being forced to look at their mean little faces. There was Sooty, a small, unstable bear who threatened everyone who crossed his path with his allegedly 'magic' wand — obviously some sort of primitive phallic symbol backing up a tremendous Napoleon complex. And there were the Woodentops, a horrific mutant nuclear family of skittles who went about their daily round of domestic drudgery with amazing placidity, never seeming to notice the terrible trick that Nature had played on them.

None of these heroes spoke; they moved stiffly and mutely across the small screen, their strings shimmering. They were *so* shoddy, and they had *such* pretensions to quiet quality, it was pathetic. Their depressingly dull actions were described by an *incredible* voice, probably several but staying in the mind as one: a prewar, Home Counties upper-middle *trill, well into the nineteen sixties.* The 'minds', if they can really be called that, behind children's TV, were so *scared*, and so *stopped*; they could not show the actual children *they* would have considered ideal as role models for others, because by the Sixties it would have been socially unacceptable to parade upper-middle children as the Chosen Ones — and yet it was just as unacceptable to *them* to show the kind of child who was the British norm, who outnumbered the upper-middle child three to one: the working-class baby beast, in all its slack-jawed, jammy-smeared glory. To show the working-class child as *the norm* would have been *to set a bad example*, and so the alternative, upsetting and exciting no one — what else is running a white Western society about? – was to show this endless parade of voiceless, boring, neither man nor beast freaks.

If you read books, as an amazing one in two hundred working-class children actually do, you read about the first cousins of these wimps: Noddy, a sort of grinning, kerb-crawling Cecil Rhodes, forever getting up against it with the marauding gollywog population, and Rupert the Bear, with his bad acid world — forever falling through traps into catacombs and being kidnapped by mythical beasts — and his Go To Hell trousers, the black and yellow check ones that he never seemed to change. On the *Daily Express* children's page he still appears in tight-assed profile with his wooden sword and shield, apeing the neurotically normal Norman soldier on the *Express* front page, a defender of the British bear's way of life.

Later you got the Public School Promised Land – Bunter, Jennings, Mallory Towers, St Claire's – savage separatism of expectations at a tender age. At eight I literally wept myself to sleep at least once a week, knowing I would never ever attend a midnight feast.

The public school stories which I pined over in the Sixties were written in the Fifties, and these were the last boarding school entertainments aimed at children, although the qualities of kitsch and corporate cruelty inherent in the system would make themselves attractive to 1980s theatre audiences in the shape of *Daisy Pulls It Off* and *Another Country*. The new Big Lie was that it was *working-class* teenagers whose lives were one long round of gaiety – though of course there has always been only a tiny section of the youth of every class who actually have the guts to have a good time – and in the late Sixties the first solid below-stairs school romp started. '5C', showcased first in the situation comedy *Please Sir!* and later *The Fenn Street Gang* were an unlikely collection of studs, starlets, simpletons and plaster saints running wild – or rather, running *mild* – within the confines of a – shock, horreur! – secondary modern. They were poor but honest, very inner-city Hovis; old morals in new hotpants. The girls clung onto their virginity for grim death, this the be-all and end-all of their existence; the boys protected the weak (i.e. the girls). No one had sex, or stole, or fought, although they did occasionally tease the janitor – live fast, die young. They were pure pantomime.

Although the Fenn Street Gang were alleged fifteen-year-olds played by grubby, buxom late-twenties actors, it *was* the first time that English working-class schoolkids had been portrayed en masse, give or take a *To Sir With Love* here or there. But by 1976 the comprehensivization of Britain was as complete as it would ever be, and the small screen was set for the state school saga par excellence – *Grange Hill*. 'The Battle of Waterloo may have been won on the playing fields of Eton,' proclaimed an official of the National Union of Teachers once, 'but the Battle of Goose Green was won in the playground of Grange Hill.' *Grange Hill* became more than a snazzy, slick sit-comic-drama for the pre-adults; it came to symbolize all that was right – or wrong, depending on which side you wore your political conscience – with the comprehensive education system.

The *Daily Mail*, for example, still in mourning for the grammar schools, saw any juvenile crime committed on the premises of a state school as a 'Grange Hill type' dastardly deed. But the *Mail* was guilty of not being able to see the wood for its widow's weeds – *Grange Hill* possessed an infinitely more moral outlook on the world than most of the programmes that the censorious wrinklies would be gawping at a few hours after lights out. The villain of the piece, one Gripper Stebson – Attila the Acned – was the embodiment of malignant adolescence – a bully, a racist, a thicko – and it was painfully obvious that sooner or later good would triumph over Gripper as sure as night followed day. What really *was* wrong with *Grange Hill* was that it was too idealized, it being impossible to depict the banality, laziness and cunning of your typical – state or private – schoolchild without looking as though you were putting them down. *Grange Hill* was beautifully acted, sympathetically crafted to act as a sort of walking, talking agony column to help worried, watching tinies with all their problems from bad skin to unrequited love for Sir or Miss; but it was probably much less 'realistic' than *Tom Brown's Schooldays* had been in its time (which would actually have made a great video nasty – *Flashman, Zombie Flesh Roaster*). Glottal stops and realism do not always go hand in glove, still a common miscomprehension.

In the Sixties, what Stan Lee once called 'the nowhere world of comic books' was annexed by the hippies. It is strange that the heads, with their amorality and pacifism, were attracted to the clean-limbed powerhouses of Marvel and DC – maybe their minds were blown by the crazy threads.

The only superhero served up to a mass audience in the Sixties was Batman, and even then the adventures of Himself and his bizarre green-knickered ward were played strictly for laughs – with Batman looking like the Before part of a Playtex girdle ad it could hardly have been otherwise – but in the Seventies things changed. Superheroes were revamped for the small screen, and new ones were invented — the pacifist psycho of Kung Fu, the six million dollar bionic boy, girl and goat all enjoying massive ratings until they let their dreams of big screen stardom get the better of them and moved on to lesser things.

At first the old superheroes, though prime time fixtures for as long as they lasted, were strictly little leaguers — the Jolly Green Psycho (a nod to the success of the vigilante flicks — *Dirty Hulky*?) and Lynda Carter as the Woman with the Rope and a Stars and Stripes corset (Wonderwoman had something for everyone — a strong, para-assertive female lead for the feminists and miles of thigh and inches of cleavage for lechers and lovers of beauty) — very much small beer compared to the blockbuster that was even now hurtling from Krypton to Planet Earth. The Superman films were a sharp, spell-blinding trilogy in which the caped crusader (played to perfection by Christopher Reeve) grew up, got orphaned, got a job, fell in love, lost his powers, slept with Pamela Stephenson, conquered the evil side of himself and called it a day.

But it was not until the advent of the *Star Wars* saga that all ground rules of children's folklore were completely rewritten. Soon it became obligatory for every last cheapo cartoon series in the American-speaking world to include a robot who practically wore a sandwich board saying I AM A FASTIDIOUS ENGLISH FAGGOT, and/or a cylindrical wisecracking little sidekick speaking in a bewitching tongue of peeps and bleeps.

From now on the shadows of C-3PO and R2-D2 would hover over the lives of short people everywhere.

The story of *Star Wars*, and of the sequels, *The Empire Strikes Back* and *Return Of The Jedi*, is basically a Good *v.* Evil one. Not again! I hear you beg and plead. Just for once could there not be a children's story involving Apathy *v.* Evil, or even Cynical Mercenary Opportunism *v.* Evil? But no, baby, not yet. Instead, Luke Skywalker, 'a simple farm boy' living on the draggy desert planet of Tatooine (Smallsville in Space) gets to join the Rebel Alliance and fight the Evil Empire, represented most odiously by the man-machine Darth Vader who, it eventually transpires, was once the heroic Jedi Knight Anakin Skywalker — Luke's daddy! To fight him, Luke has to learn the ancient ways of the Jedi, no cakewalk.

Like everything else, there were the usual sensible theories about the *Star Wars* saga being a CIA plot, etc. The EVIL EMPIRE *v.* the REBEL ALLIANCE − the Warsaw Pact *v.* NATO! It is true that Ronald Reagan once called the Soviet Union 'the evil empire' in a key policy speech to a hallful of rabid Christians, but this was a good five years after the first *Star Wars* film hit the screen; it can hardly be blamed on George Lucas that Mr Reagan's speechwriters are a pack of plagiaristic hysterics. On the contrary, there was a lot of the liberal ethos about the films. The Rebel Alliance was composed of monsters, mutants, machines, blacks, princesses and petty criminals − anyone with their heart in the right place welcome. You didn't have to be John Wayne to be a hero − you could look like a teddy bear (the Ewoks) or a dustbin (R2-D2). Luke himself spends a good deal of the first film running around in a sheer white blouson that makes him look as though he has come fresh to the fray from a shopping spree at Laura Ashley. The mega-men are on the bad side: the Stormtroopers, the very tall Darth Vader (played by the muscle man David Prowse), the bounty hunters (space mercenaries who will work for anyone wicked). The title of the third film was even changed from *Revenge* of the Jedi to *Return*, the proposed title eventually rejected as possessing the wrong vibes (man).

You have only to look at Mr Lucas, the great Creator, to know that he was a youngblood in the 1960s − like all the so-called movie brats, he bears an unfortunate physical resemblance to Charles Manson − and you have only to be exposed to 'the Force', the power that is central to the Star Wars story, to realize that the philosophy behind the films comes from closer to Haight-Ashbury than West Point.

The Force, which Luke Skywalker learns to use in the course of the trilogy, is very reminiscent of that spiritual hula hoop of the early Seventies, Kung Fu: very mystic, very non-specific, very defensive. Like Kung Fu it combines the attractions of pacifism and extreme violence; Luke, like the David Carradine character Cane, is a sweet, gentle manboy who will only fight when pushed to the point of no return − luckily for the fight fans, he gets pushed there pretty regularly.

The ways of the Force are taught to Luke by the most adorable character created in the history of the cinema, the Jedi Master, Yoda. Yoda is a tiny, cantankerous green being, strongly resembling Lord Wilson in both facial feature and temperament. 'Unlearn, unlearn!' Yoda yells at Luke endlessly, in a bid to break down his pride and self-confidence which Master Yoda considers misplaced. He sits on Luke's shoulders, complaining bitterly all the time, while the unfortunate young Jedi jogs himself stupid in a bid to make his body a finely tuned conductor of the Force. Yet when Yoda takes to his bed and hovers between life and death halfway through *Return of the Jedi* — 'Sick I've become. Yes. Old and weak. When nine hundred years you reach, look as good you will not. Soon I will rest for ever. Earned it I have' — there is not a dry eye in the house. Watching the grumbling green goblin gasp his last, one thinks irresistibly of *Camille*.

Part of the reason why the Star Wars films were not hellish to an adult, even when forced by a besotted four-year-old to sit through a particular one for the eighteenth time, was because they contained so many references to old Hollywood, and it was entertaining to see stock situations beefed up with breathtaking special effects and mutant make-up. George Lucas must have been born in the back row of the movies; 'Klaatu Brada Nikto' the Thing From Outer Space says as an icebreaker to the earthling in *It Came From Outer Space* (1953) and exactly thirty years later both Klaatu and Nikto are brought to scaly, monstrous life at the court of Jabba the Hutt (no oil painting himself).

The confrontation between Luke and his bad daddy is very *High Noon*, and the exclusion of the droids from the Tatooine bar — 'We don't serve their sort!' — is rather *Gentleman's Agreement*. The sex and cruelty banquets at the court of the Hutt resemble Cecil B. DeMille's sumptuous sin wallows, while Luke Skywalker's early appearance while working on his uncle's farm, getting up from the teatable in a tantrum after being told that he must stay and help out rather than go off to the Space Academy with his chums — 'Where are you going, Luke?' 'It looks like I'm going nowhere!' — is James Dean in the extreme. The smuggling yobbo Han Solo's habit of turning around and telling the haughty Princess Leia 'What you need is a darn good kissing!' whenever she acts assertively is pure Tracey and Hepburn, while the cute comic relief of the droids — the pessimistic, hypochondriac C-3PO, the pugnacious, optimistic R2-D2 — resembles nothing so much as a cosmic *Odd Couple*.

It was a *World*, the thing George Lucas created, and like an iceberg only a tiny part of it was ever seen.. A spark of genius, working its tail off — 'I was thinking about *Star Wars* all through *American Graffiti*,' Mr Lucas has said, 'and I began writing it in January 1973 — eight hours a day, five days a week, from then until March 1976 when we began shooting.' Postwar children's culture had always been so *shoddy*, so *insulting* — so *little* time and energy obviously went into the creation of such giants as Muffin and Andy Pandy — as though a dismissive adult had knocked it out in a tea break before getting back to the *important* stuff, the quiz shows and the potter's wheel. George Lucas was obsessed with his subject, and perhaps children sensed this, and chose to reward him accordingly.

The Star Wars saga was executed with such total conviction because of the time, imagination, hard labour, *the desire to return* that Lucas had invested for literally years in creating his private world; what appeared on the screen were fleeting, fabulous glimpses of a mind-made universe that was backed up by data mountains of fantastic detail. For example, Lucas said, 'Let there be Stormtroopers'. All that got to the screen of the Imperial Stormtroopers were thugs in white latex gear, their faces hidden behind shiny white gas masks, who ran about in packs shooting at the heroes. But in Mr Lucas' mind they went from cradle (or 'hatchery') to grave (or at least to the Stormtroopers rest camp on the holiday planet of Sochi), a group of genetically identical clones with no human rights and no names, the property of the Emperor. Every stage of their development was present in his files and his mind.

And there were Stormtroopers. And Lucas saw the Stormtroopers, that they were rotten to the core. And he said, let there be Jawas and Tusken Raiders and Hoth Wampas and the Rancour and the Sarlaac that dwells in the

Great Pit of Carkoon — and the Big Bad Wolf went by the board.

Then there was ET, the wrinkled enigma from another universe; part God, part prune. He broke box office records and hearts for a relatively short time in the history of the world, and if you go into any toyshop in the land you will find ET dolls, ET scrapbooks and ET toilet plungers, a veritable ET mountain, all gathering the sad dust of anti-climax, of hype's morning after. ET turned out to be a better-looking Adam Ant on the grand scale, but he did testify once and for all that postwar children's culture, the apex of which had once been a bit of hacked-about balsa wood jittering from a string (pace Andy Pandy), was now a mega-million pound industry and the best place to be from a bullion point of view — *all the films which break the box office these days are films aimed at children*. The critics complain that Mr Steven Spielberg and Mr Lucas do not make films for adults any more, but why should they? Why should children not have clever directors working solely for them? Adults do; and you do not hear tinies running around writing to the newspapers complaining that Wim Wenders never makes movies about the antics of cute aliens.

These new movie brattytales have completely obliterated the old fairytales; the fairytales have been flung to the feminists, who revamp them and feed them to each other featuring Snow White as a black lesbian activist and suchforth. The genteel, cucumber sandwich-eating *Watch With Mother* puppets probably lie mouldering in some musty BBC basement, too; they have been replaced with matey, knowing, prole-speaking dummies.

The only meek and mild puppet on the modern scene is Orville, the pathologically shy and self-effacing green baby duck, much given to cheap emotion and copious weeping, pretty much the Johnny Ray of the hand-held set. At the other extreme you have the mute vandals; Spit the Dog and Emu. The ignorant 'Spit' merely lives up to his name — but the Emu is another kettle of broken bones altogether. A frenzied, staring beast of many unlikely hues, the Emu is a tarred and feathered chainsaw massacre — really nothing more than an excuse for his master, one Rod Hull, to throttle male talk show hosts he envies (Michael Parkinson, after the Emu had tried repeatedly to bite him on his vasectomy scar, said to Rod Hull while the cameras were off them 'If you do that again I'll smash your face in') and put his hand (cleverly located inside Emu's horrible hollow head) up the skirts of female TV presenters he fancies (his televised sexual assault of the regal Selina Scott was a national disgrace. At breakfast time, too).

The best modern puppet is Zippy of *Rainbow*, a cute being of indeterminate origins − he rather resembles a rusty soup ladle, and he has an open zip for a mouth. His voice is harsh, and he rants and complains constantly − when he goes too far, his friends simply zip him up. Other charmers are Mooncat, Duncan the Dragon, Cosmo and Dibbs the dog-monkey monsters − all used to illustrate the problems and weaknesses of small children, such as clumsiness, self-doubt, over-sensitivity, bossiness, contrariness and hysteria. They speak in lowly born, vaguely Croydon accents (apart from the adorable Cosmo, who is a Geordie) and have been known to employ irony and sarcasm (the highest form of humour) − a long way from the Wooden-tops.

The archetypal disrespectful dummy of humble origin, the most successful and unattractive, is Roland Rat, the 'Superstar' of TV-AM and BBC. He is often drunk by nine in the morning. He is full of himself. He is conceited and amazingly cheap-looking; he seems to have been made from oddments garnered by a rummager through the bins of the garment district, with just the kind of fur that might have made an urban lower middle-class American Jewish girl of the 1950s her first showy coat. Yet he did what Peter Jay, Angela Rippon, David Frost, Anna Ford and Robert Kee, with all their huge swollen heads and salaries, could not do. He got the inflated, failure-prone TV-AM *ratings*. He literally changed its fortunes, bringing the viewing figures from under one million to over two million, finally outstripping the BBC breakfast show (to whom he had first been offered).

Constructed by, written for, and spoken for by the hustler-about-town David Claridge, the boy behind the short-lived, sensational dance/sex/night club Skin 2, Roland was apparently conceived as a rat because DC likes rodents, believing that 'they most effectively suggest working-class gutsiness'. Soon after the Rat's arrival the horribly named 'Famous Five' presenters started to get the message and slope off to browner, low-profile pastures. If he had been put together with the sole intent of making the self-adoring quintet realize just how *resistible* they were to the breakfast-bolting nation, just how expendable they were to the money men, Mr Rat could not have carried out his task better. Suggestive, cynical, common as muck, he was what the People in their infinite wisdom chose over the 'Mission to Explain' that Peter Jay proposed in *his* infinite, Godlike wisdom at the outset of the fiasco.

His Ratship is about as far as a dummy could devolve from the well-bred, mindless Muffin the Mule. He assumes that his audience is vulgar and knowing, despite its tender years; Roland has seen a few video nasties in his time and assumes that his fans — 'My Ratfans' — have too. The matter of children watching sick video films at home became a moral panic during the Enemy-Within Eighties; the sickest thing about it seemed not the fact that the children were getting hold of these things, but that in several recorded cases their parents were *encouraging* them, *inducing* them to watch the wretched products. Watch With Mother — *Cannibal Holocaust*. Sterilization, preferably on the spot, preferably with a rusty old tin can, would seem the most reasonable, reformist course of re-education suitable for these impossibly spiritually impoverished people; but one really should not be shocked. As I have said, adults have always enjoyed feeding children grisly garbage and calling it entertainment, from Grimm to *Driller Killer*. People try out a lot of their nastinesses on children, treating them in ways they would not dare treat adults, even though children are supposedly the most sheltered members of our society.

Neurotic people are still drawn to the creation of children's culture, though these days the illnesses are on the grand scale. Being a child is still a wretched experience from which no sensitive person ever *really* recovers, but culturally things are a lot less barren and bland. Many more people of much more brain are bent on diverting you from your miserable lot; and insofar as the process of being 'entertained' sits gracefully on anyone, it does on you. The less one knows, the more excuse one has to sit there imitating a sponge, sucking up the sad fantasies of others.

Only a Game

Britain invented Torvill and Dean because Diana and Charles could not reasonably be expected to get married every year. The function that Jayne and Christopher fulfilled was exactly that of the other lovable comic duo, Spencer and Windsor – a no-sex British love story to tie a granny knot in the heartstrings of (hopefully) the world, and conclusive proof to Johnny Foreigner that 'we' still know how to put on a show of pomp and circumstance better than any other nation. Both double acts inspired the sentimental smugness that is the most underestimated aspect of the great British character.

It was entirely fitting that the people of these islands should tug a collective forelock and confer royal status on their Royal Highnesses the Prince and Princess of Nottingham, for ice skating – with its meticulously preordained choreography, fanciful dress and movements that consist of wandering around in apparently pointless, ever-decreasing circles – is closer to the Trooping of the Colour than to a sport. The competitors never make eye contact, the scoring is entirely subjective, beauty and points awarded for artistic merit are in the eye of the beholder. Applause or a raspberry are the only possible responses.

It is hardly a sport at all. This accounts for its current popularity. Almost every sport that has increased in popularity since the war has been hardly a sport at all. Just as the traditional industries – steel, shipbuilding, coal mining – have been in steady decline in modern times, so the traditional sports have similarly been on the slide to the scrapheap of history.

Snooker is to the sporting life what the microchip is to industry — new fangled, insubstantial, the shape of things to come whether you like it or lump it. The immobile melodrama of the sedentary sports — snooker, darts, is perfectly suited to television, the medium which has been an even greater benefactor to the sedentary sports than Benson & Hedges.

The corollary of the rise of sports which are barely sports at all is that there has been a dramatic increase in the number of sportsmen who bear no resemblance whatsoever to what we expect a sportsman to look like. It is impossible to watch a sedentary sport without experiencing wave after wave of nausea, caused by the sight of a witless blubber mountain with a dart in one hand and a vat of ale in the other, or some snooker-playing spiv puffing away like a commercial for lung cancer and dipping his greedy snout in a trough of vodka in between red balls.

But it is not only the sedentary sports that are populated by people who do not look the part. American football is bursting out all over with men who would not look out of their natural habitat in a fairground sideshow — and with the increase of Human Growth Hormone abuse in the sport, a fairground sideshow will, for many of them, soon be the only work they can get.

American football players are crumbling like derelict tower blocks. They are building up their muscles with an illegal substance called Human Growth Hormone, which inflates their muscles to such huge proportions that when they take a hard fall their bones literally snap under the strain.

'We are seeing significantly more catastrophic knee, ankle and elbow injuries in football,' said Dr Eugene Luckstead of the American Academy of Pediatrics. 'Many of these injuries are being kept secret. No one is keeping statistics any more.' HGH can add up to four stone to an athlete's weight while adding not an inch to his waistline. It is available for one thousand dollars — a very small investment compared to the massive amounts of money to be made in American football — for a course of treatment lasting six to ten weeks. Extracted from the pituitary gland during autopsy, it does not merely increase the size of the biceps but stimulates the liver to send out messenger molecules saying GROW to almost every cell in the body. Used to excess, HGH causes acromegaly, a disease that owes everything to overactivity of the pituitary gland, resulting in overgrowth of bones, especially those in the hands, feet, jaw and skull, resulting in what American sportsmen refer to as the Frankenstein Look.

Robert Goldman, a researcher in sports medicine and author of *Death in the Locker Room*, says, 'Human Growth Hormone is the drug of the near future. At the moment HGH is quite rare and expensive. It is needed to treat children who are deficient in the hormone and must be given it to reach normal size. *The abominable thing about the black market in HGH is that fully grown athletes are stealing from these children.* Thanks to a recent scientific breakthrough, however, this drug has been synthesized in the laboratory and will probably be on the market by the end of the year. I presume the price will plummet, as happened in the case of pocket calculators. If so, athletes will rush to buy, because it has become an obsession with many of them.'

HGH mania, Goldman believes, is caused by the fact that in pro sports an athlete needs to be only slightly stronger and bigger than his opponent to win. An advantage of just 3 per cent body strength can mean the difference between a weightlifter's Olympic medal being silver or gold. If an entire football team takes HGH, Mr Goldman says, it will have an overwhelming 10 per cent advantage over teams which do not use Human Growth Hormone.

He polled nearly 200 professional sportsmen, asking them, 'If I had a magic drug so fantastic it would let you win every event you entered, but would kill you after five years – would you take it?' To which over 50 per cent of those polled replied in the affirmative. 'The evidence suggests athletes will take anything to win,' Mr Goldman says, 'especially those in big money team sports. Some basketball players and footballers earn up to a million dollars a year, and even the average professional team player in many sports makes over 100,000 dollars per annum.' The sports physician Dr Arnold Mandell says that team coaches believe American football is best played in a state of controlled anger, which is why use of amphetamines is so widespread in the sport. Says Mr Goldman, 'When it is a matter of winning or losing, a trainer will give any kind of drug to any kind of player.'

A group of Californian bodybuilders produced the *Underground Steroid Handbook For Men And Women* just in time for the Los Angeles Olympics: it details the availability of banned drugs, effects, dosages and side effects of illegal drugs, such as beards on girls and the aforementioned Frankenstein Look. But the authors' message is clear — Victory Through Drugs. The entry under Human Growth Hormone drooled, 'Wow, this is great stuff! This is the only drug that can remedy bad genetics, as it will make anybody grow. People who use it can expect to gain 30 to 40 pounds of muscle in ten weeks if they can eat about 10,000 calories per day. A few side effects can occur, however. It may elongate your chin, feet and hands. Diabetes in teenagers is possible with it. We have heard of a powerlifter getting a heart attack on HGH. It is the biggest gamble that an athlete can take, as the side effects are irreversible. Even with all that, we LOVE the stuff.'

It is not just world-class athletes going for gold — whether in bullion or medallion form — who are prepared to do their bodies grotesque, irreparable, sometimes fatal harm. This is the age of the Amateur Wreck. Those most in danger are the old and unfit and, conversely, the young and gifted. A talented child pushes — or more likely, by parents and coach is pushed — towards perfection and ends up with some permanent injury, looking for a day job. A menopausal amateur sportsman strains and sweats after the Holy Grail of eternal youthful fitness and the next of kin ends up collecting on the insurance.

In the Fifties it was believed that exercise could do one nothing but good — no one could foresee that the day would come when child gymnasts would be developing osteochondritis, caused by overuse of the spine which leads eventually to permanent back damage, or that porcine middle-aged men would be out jogging to an early slimline grave. No one could foresee the day, but — in tennis and swimming and athletics, with eleven-year-old ex-gymnasts who have permanent back damage, teenage footballers who will never turn professional because they have developed Osgood-Schlatter's disease, caused by overuse of the knee, with four deaths in Marathon races in Britain alone in the last year, with dozens of fatal heart attacks on the squash court — that day is here. In the age of death and disablement for all, even the amateurs take sport in deadly earnest. It has been a very long time since it was the taking part that mattered most.

That sport can seriously damage your health is only news to those sportspersons with amateur status — professional boxers, of course, have been making a living by becoming walking wounded for over a hundred years, though, ironically enough, never more so than since the end of bare knuckle fighting.

Boxing, twice on the verge of oblivion, has had two saviours — the Marquess of Queensberry in the 1860s and Cassius Clay a century later. The Marquess saved the sport from being banned, and Muhammad Ali (né Mr Clay) saved it from being boring beyond all limits of human endurance. That Mr Ali did not live happily ever after is the direct fault of the Marquess.

For since the Marquess of Queensberry wrote his celebrated rulebook in 1867 — at a time when the blood and gore of bare knuckle fighting had put boxing in grave danger of being made illegal — boxers have worn gloves. While boxing gloves greatly reduce the chances of a boxing match resembling a video nasty full of spurting blood and multi-coloured bruises, gloves, as well as saving the sport from being outlawed, made it what it is today — a short cut to brain damage.

For boxing gloves, though they reduce the possibility of the torn flesh of superficial injuries, are not designed to protect the head of the man being hit — they are designed to protect the hands of the man doing the hitting. Knockouts were rare in the days of bare knuckle fighting — now they are routine. Gloves are weapons, no more or less, which much increase the chances of brain injury. Mr Ali — the greatest boxer of all time and a sportsman who deserved a better sport than boxing — has the Marquess of Queensberry to thank for his heartbreakingly laborious thought patterns and slurred, stumbling speech. Before the end of the century boxing will have to go back to bare knuckles or be banned − and a return to bare knuckles would surely eventually lead to the same conclusion.

Probably the greatest of all arguments for banning boxing is the audience it attracts. No young people − all too busy learning a martial art or painting their toenails. Few blacks (outside the ring). No sentient girls, only middle-aged bits of fluff who look like Miss TV Times 1957. The *noise* that comes from their wretched throats indicates that, with a boxing crowd, brain damage is also in the head of the beholder. No half-hearted amendments − thumbless gloves, conscientious medical boards not afraid to revoke a fighter's licence, referees who believe that the mob getting its money's worth is *not* the first priority − can ever obliterate the masturbatory sadism in that noise a fight crowd makes, no amount of cheery endorsements for cat food by your Henry can ever drown that sound.

What finally differentiates boxing from all the other sports is that *no one who could do anything else would do it*. It is this which makes the sport so inherently insulting to anyone who steps into the ring; young technocrats become runners and boys with degrees in Russian choose to play for Spurs, but no one who could do anything but box would box.

(The *Rocky* saga pandered to the Old World myth that a poor boy from the wrong side of the tracks could *only* break out in the direction of crime or boxing. Neither option really cuts it as a credible YOP scheme in the modern world − the former will get you a Met bullet in the cranium for carrying a replica Luger into some suburban post office and the latter will get you brain damage before you get your first grey hair. Neither is exactly the Promised Land for even the most witless oik.

No, a poor boy from the wrong side of the tracks whose first million is still a twinkle in his bank manager's balance sheet would do better to forget fighting his way to the top − rather he should simply sit back on his toches and tap out a screenplay while his wife works as an usherette to support him.

That's what Rocky did . . .

In the trials of Rocky, our hero got the girl and lost the girl, got the world championship and lost the world championship, got the happiness and lost the happiness, got and lost everything but brain damage and it was all quite touching. But the so-called Italian Stallion made *his* megabucks acting, writing and directing − possibly the three least physical activities known to man − while stoking the fire to roast that hoary old chestnut: if a poor boy wants to get out of this place, he gotta do it with one fist of iron and the other of steel.

During the hungry years, while Mr Stallone sat at home on his grossly overdeveloped fanny, what would his reaction have been, I wonder, had some helpful soul suggested that the way out of his low rent life was putting on the gloves and stepping into the ring? By the time of *Rocky*, the fight game had become happiest as a mawkish memory, another sentimental stitch in tinsel town's rich tapestry.)

Naples is one of the poorest cities in Europe, with one million unemployed. In the summer of 1984, the church bells rang all night and fireworks lit the sky. In scenes reported by observers to be more hysterical than Liberation Day, Italy's World Cup victory and the city's visit by the Pope combined − combined! − the people lit torches, dived into the sea, danced until dawn and then went to early morning Mass to give thanks.

For after forty-three days of negotiations, Diego Maradona, five feet four inch twenty-three-year-old Argentinian, formerly of Argentinos Juniors of Buenos Aires and Barcelona, allegedly the greatest footballer in the world, was on his way to Napoli for a transfer fee of five million pounds put up by a combine of Italian banks. Street traders sold Maradona treacle toffee, Maradona religious icons and Maradona sausages. Weeping with joy, the Neapolitans showed the street traders the colour of their lire.

Maradona was equally over the moon. His three-year contract with Napoli gave him everything but the Malvinas − £740,000 per annum plus 15 per cent of the five million pounds transfer fee, a villa, a car (and a car for his girlfriend), a percentage of the takings at Napoli's home games, fifteen first-class return tickets a year to visit the old folks in BA plus a promise from Napoli to buy a brace of Argentinian internationals to make the stocky little forward feel at home. The people of Napoli thought they had a bargain.

Rather than being a shining example of football's ruddy health, the Maradona transfer to Napoli was indicative of just how infirm the game had become. The hysteria of the Neapolitans was an act of faith that flew in the face of all the evidence. It could only happen in a Catholic country: Napoli is the Lourdes of soccer.

For there had been almost as much excitement in 1982 when Maradona was transferred from Argentinos Juniors to Barcelona. Two years later the Bimbo d'Oro – Golden Boy – had been reduced to common or garden bimbo status, blotted out of game after game with the most vicious of marking resulting in long spells of injury and suspension (after retaliating when it all became too much), mediocrity and depression. *A player like Mr Maradona is simply too good to be allowed to play*. As it was in España, so it will be in Italia.

Football is a sport with a great future behind it. The game's golden era dates from the abolition of the maximum wage in 1961 (when players could only earn up to £20 a week) to the taming of George Best, the years between the quasi-amateurism of the baggy-trousered solid citizens and the mean-minded, dull-witted man-marking of the modern drones, coached beyond all inspiration and instinct. The years of the Spurs double side showing Europe how, of England winning the World Cup against the Germans – in red shirts, Mr Wilson smiled – of the genesis of Mr Shankly's Liverpool, the prime time of Pele and Eusebio and of Manchester United rising like a phoenix from the funeral pyre of the Munich air disaster. Matt Busby had a dream. One man, more than any other, made it come true.

In 1961 Bob Bishop, the manager of a Belfast boys' team called Boyland, watched his team get beat 4–2 by Cregah Boys' Team. A fifteen-year-old boy called George Best was playing for Cregah. Bob Bishop was also the Northern Ireland scout for Manchester United. He telephoned United's manager and told Matt Busby, 'I think I've found a genius.'

George Best put football on the Pop map, as celebrated

for his blondes, boutiques and Beatled hair-do as his phenomenal football skills. When he had a house built in Bramhall, a Manchester suburb, Pierre Trudeau flew in for the party. He was the archetypal professional footballer of the Sixties — his career coincided and lasted as long as the decade. Ten years after Bob Bishop caught sight of him and cried *eureka!* Jean Rook wrote in her *Daily Sketch* column, 'Isn't it time somebody told George Best he's getting far too big for his football boots? Or am I the only ex-fan who's sick of watching young twinkle ankles treating other people like they were the ball? George, you're gorgeous, nobody doubts it. Mr Fab Feet himself. The sexiest thing that ever slid inside a soccer shirt two sizes too tight. You're also becoming a great big-headed, baby-faced bore. Grow up and belt up, why don't you? Just switch it off a bit, EH?'

The players' infatuation with what they perceived as the pop lifestyle — the long hair and the kissing (it would be interesting to know just who exactly was the first player to kiss another, and what the reaction of the crowd and the other players was), the late Sixties boomtown hysteria of adultery and alcoholism and gambling and bankruptcy — peaked in the early Seventies when it became clear that Mr Best had finally been bettered by the bottle. Soon the boutiques were closing and the bubble cuts were left on the cutting room floor. George Best was used as a bogeyman to scare the trusting children of football into good clean living off the field.

The ironic corollary of this was that it became unacceptable even to attempt to *play* in the Best fashion. Flair was outlawed, resulting in a generation of drones, drilled into the ground by their coaches. The Goody-Goody Artisan syndrome was embodied by Kevin Keegan, a credit to his game (not to mention his species), but he was the *only* annotation in the profit margin of this new ethic that gripped the game. Of course Mr Keegan's game had flashes of brilliance — and Best's work rate and tackling were the two most underrated facets of his game — but when George hung up his boots, the fundamentals of the sport changed for ever. *Après* Best, football players, instead of striving to be artists, were not only content but expected — *ordered!* — to be workmanlike artisans.

Paradoxically, though the parable of the Bad Boy from Belfast successfully scared football players into the lifestyle of commuters and the artistry of mules, football *managers* (short-back-and-sides workadaddies in the Sixties when Best was being snapped sharing a joke with Susan George on some Majorcan beach) woke up one morning and asked themselves collectively, 'What am I *missing*?' As the players became conscientious citizens the managers took on the roles of the game's wild men with relish; their balding pates forever gleaming with sweaty anticipation, gold medallions clanking excitedly on their suntanned pot bellies as they abandon home and hearth to set up what is invariably dubbed a 'love nest' with some divorced Blackburn beautician.

While the managers feather their love nests, the mood in the boardroom is gloomy. Clubs have come within spitting distance of going to the wall, but have so far always been saved at the eleventh hour by some benevolent benefactor who made a mint in wet fish. Yet the day cannot be too far away when a club's bankruptcy will not be avoided by the timely appearance of some frozen pea magnate.

Now that the bottom has fallen out of the domestic transfer market the only place a club can collect a multi-million pound fortune in exchange for its best boys is Italy. Only a country as poor as Italy can afford to have the total, suicidal disregard for seven-figure sums that they are willing to spend on luring the cream of two continents to their league. Napoli had an overdraft of four million pounds before they spent a cent on Maradona.

Back home on the terraces the mood is ugly if too often overstated. Football, more than any other sport, reflects the multi-racial nature of the country — no other game has an international squad with a higher percentage of black players — yet the caged crowds taunt, jeer and throw bunches of bananas at black players, which is bad news for everyone but the greengrocer. Football is not only the national game, it is also the National Front game. In recent seasons dwindling crowds gave rise to the hope that soon a hooligan would have to run fifty metres before he found someone to stab, but with Chelsea, Sheffield Wednesday and Newcastle all newly promoted to the First Division, and all bringing huge away support up with them, this slender hope for love and peace has been dashed.

On the pitch itself − that area of the footballing world that has become so easy to overlook − there is talk of revolution. The football France played to cruise to the 1984 European Championship was widely hailed as a breathtaking innovation which would save the game from dying under the weight of formations, functions and tactics. The French manager, Michel Hidalgo, certainly talked a great game. 'The most beautiful image of football', he told John Goodbody in *World Soccer*, 'is the football of childhood, practised by boys of eight to fourteen years old. At fifteen or sixteen, one begins to calculate, one wants to play like grown-ups. One loses generosity and innocence.'

But the generosity and innocence of the French side as they struggled to victory in the final of the European Championship against the irascible talents of the Spanish could not obscure the fact that, for all the dreamy talk about a return to the beautiful basics of the playground, France had a third-rate defence, a first-rate midfield and a second-rate attack. They merely played to their strengths − the silky skills of Tigana, Giresse and Platini. Hardly the Second Coming − even *England* might have given them a run for their francs − but then the Lost Tribe of Soccer very much needs a saviour. It is getting desperate.

Meanwhile back in Naples as Diego Maradona and Jorge Orazio Cysterzpiller, his business manager, arrived in town to an ecstatic reception, Luther Blisset, last year's Bimbo d'Oro, was quietly slipping out the back door and Father Armando Guidetti was complaining that the hysteria around Maradona's arrival was unreasonable and to be condemned. Why not, he suggested, spend those millions on something that would uplift the masses onto a higher spiritual plane? Why not something like the Nobel Prize?

A fan who had camped out for weeks joining in the festivities heatedly put him in his place.

'Can you eat a Nobel Prize?' he demanded. 'Does a Nobel Prize drive you mad with joy? Anyway,' the unknown fan said, 'what *is* a Nobel Prize?'

The media would like every pro tennis player to be a psycho, a nympho or a Sappho — preferably all three. Though most players do not warrant a salacious tabloid seeding, the comings and goings-on of enough of them do tend to make the sport more familiar to the front page than the back, more of a circus than a Circuit.

While Billie-Jean King awoke the libido of the mass media's interest in tennis, it was John Patrick McEnroe who was used to strut the low rent end of the media's sense of etiquette and moral outrage — hooliganism incarnate, a walking, talking, screaming, squawking metaphor for What's Wrong With Young People Today.

Yet talk of obliterating 'bad' behaviour on court is absurd — apart from the irrefutable fact that bad behaviour equals good copy, the standard of tennis officials borders on institutionalized cretinism. The players protest, sulks and spats are, in most cases, both justified and entertaining.

There is a ridiculous focus on innocuous incidents — Jimmy Connors holding his nose to signify his distaste for an erroneous line call made all the TV evening news programmes while the rapes, murders and armed robberies of the day did not warrant even a mention in the whimsical bit at the end. Though in one respect the tennis pros bring it on themselves; they are a prissy, showily sensitive lot when it comes to their sport, demanding the quiet of the grave from the paying customers, having a blue fit if a piece of paper or a rogue pigeon wafts onto the court. If they act like delicate flowers then naturally people will expect them to smell as sweet.

Tennis is the one sport that does not have a close season. All year round, over five continents, the action never stops. Paradoxically Britain considers tennis a seasonal festivity, like Easter or Christmas, and the nation only thinks about the game in the two or three weeks at the end of June and the start of July. *This* — and not the lousy weather, lousy facilities, lousy et cetera — is the reason why the British produce exclusively rotten players. For forty-nine weeks of the year, we are just not concentrating.

But when Wimbledon rolls around, the sport takes out a block booking in the minds and media of the nation. Many burning issues have to be resolved. Which lovely young woman is the reigning men's champion in love with?

Which lovely young woman is the reigning women's champion in love with?

At Wimbledon '84 the press discovered that the bitchiness they had always suspected lurked in the powder rooms of beauty pageants was alive and scratching in the locker room of women's tennis:

Martina: 'I was happy Chris beat Hana. Hana has no respect for anyone. I don't think there is any love for Hana from any of the girls.'

Hana: 'That's just not true. I get on fine with all the girls. Except her.'

Martina: 'When Hana first came on the tour she came to me for help. I tried. Somewhere along the line she has got bitter with everyone.'

Hana: 'A lie. I never asked her for any help.'

Martina: 'I didn't see it, but I know that in Paris and at Wimbledon she has made strong-arm signs with her arms when I hit a winner. I'm supposed to have all these muscles and it's as if to say "Poor little Hana". If you listen to her, she's got all the shots and I win only because I've got big legs!'

Hana: 'I'm just saying what everyone can see! People should ask what the doctors have been doing to her!'

When the players decline to stick voodoo pins in each others effigies, the Fourth Estate are more than happy to oblige.

McEnroe, on his best behaviour throughout the 1984 tournament, had the spotlight switched from his abnormal lack of self-control to his love life. Bettina Bunge, busty blonde Bavarian baseliner, Janis Levy, luscious-lipped Cadbury Flake temptress, and Kitty Godfrey, eighty-three-year-old former women's champion, were all the transient leading ladies in fabricated 'Mac And Me' stories. If he wants to avoid the same saucy scrutiny next year he will have to revert to his old bad, mad ways – otherwise he will certainly be the subject of another clutch of arranged matings.

Hyperbole abounds around the courts of Wimbledon – Ivan Lendl was called 'Surly . . . arrogant . . . the tennis bully boy of Czechoslovakia' by the *Daily Mirror* for quietly asking a female line judge where her white stick was, while

Patti Connors — former Playmate of the Year, we were constantly reminded — put on a few pounds and had pages devoted to her allegedly expecting the imminent patter of a baby Jimbo. Mighty Martina was awakened in the middle of the night to answer questions about her platonic friendship with pouting Texan mother-of-two Judy Nelson, just because Martina is a girl with a few notches — female basketball player, sex change tennis player, lesbian literary lion — on her oversized racquet. Navratilova said she would only ever set foot in England again to play Wimbledon, and for once the players refrained from scratching each others close-set eyes out — all the best tennis players have eyes that almost touch; see Connors, McEnroe and esp. five-times Wimbledon winner, Swedish ace Sven Cyclops — to unite against a very common enemy.

'I see players very upset in the locker room,' chided Chris Evert Lloyd Reynolds Faith Etcetera. 'If you want to see great tennis, don't try to upset us. If the stories were true, I could understand the curiosity about players' personal lives. But most of the stuff isn't true. It's worse here than anywhere else and for some reason it's worse this year.'

As we have already seen, it was worse this year because Mr McEnroe had not seen a red mist since Queen's.

While the accusations about the intrusions into privacy were well grounded it was equally true that the press had been led on. Tennis players are the biggest bunch of tabloid teasers outside of those rank starlets who were once within a fifty mile radius of Prince Randy. McEnroe had a contract worth big drinks with the *Sun* (going upmarket after previous years when his inky thoughts had been exclusive to the *News of the World*), John Lloyd posed in existential misery in a lonely room to illustrate the piece in which he poured out his broken heart to the sympathetic shorthand of Noreen from the *Mirror*, the Czech bully boy of tennis was signed to Lord Rothermere's bully boys of Conservatism and the Florida Ice Dolly herself was offered a choice of advances for her autobiography — a tidy sum for her thoughts on My Life In Tennis and an even tidier sum for racy revelations of the My Love Games Off Court kind. Naturally enough she chose the second option. Basically, tennis players don't mind telling as long as they are selling.

And why not? It's a short life, which is probably why tennis players tend to be so ridiculously right-wing and self-protective. McEnroe is a supporter of Mr Reagan while Pam Shriver, despite being a relation of Democrat warhorse and Kennedy-in-law Sargent, is actively campaigning for the re-election of Bonzo's old leading man. They dress their political thoughts on the Right because they tend to earn huge amounts of money in a concentrated period of time, a taxing problem for any professional athelete.

And yet McEnroe refuses to play in South Africa (though the Czech bully boy of tennis does not), Vitas Gerulitis does good works with off-white under-privileged children, Carina Karlsson donated some of her 1984 Wimbledon prize money to 'the hungry people of the world'. Most people are only involved in sports when they are not yet adults – those exceptionally gifted souls who play on and become professionals somehow seem to keep at least a part of themselves in a childlike state where the logical world of grownups never intrudes. Even so-called 'Buster' Mottram, for horrible example, though an ex-member of the National Front spends a large part of his spare time writing songs with Kenny Lynch when, logically, he should be burning crosses on Mr Lynch's lawn.

Tennis players are mixed up all the way to the bank. It is a sport where even the mediocre can make a mint – £1300 for being knocked out in straight sets in the first round of Wimbledon, for example. A few weeks after her eighteenth birthday Andrea Jaegar became the fiftieth tennis player to become a dollar millionaire since the sport went open in 1968. At the time of Wimbledon '84 there were thirty-seven men and thirteen women who had made their first million by knocking a ball over a net in the presence of paying customers. Players who are only household names in the households of their blood relatives have made seven-figure sums out of doubles alone. Even players like Sue Barker and Anne Smith – the Who? sisters – are nearing that first million. Martina Navratilova has made over seven million, and all these figures are merely on-site prize money, winnings. They do not include endorsements, which can be more lucrative – ten times more lucrative for a top seed – than winning a Grand Slam event. Sponsorship deals for shoes, socks, shorts, shirts, racquets, headbands, wrist-bands, airlines, burger chains, fast cars and disposable razors – that's what a tennis pro's bank balance is made of.

As an unseeded player who made the quarter finals at this year's Wimbledon remarked, 'You can turn pro at four if you're good enough.' This results in many players, their cradle marks cunningly concealed by their suntans, being in the top tax bracket before they are emotionally continent. Last year Andrea Jaegar started grizzling as Mrs Lloyd took her to the cleaners, and this year Fraulein Stefi Graf was making with the waterworks as she went out to that sizeable All England sweatshop, Miss Durie.

The pressures of a sport with no close season, of the travelling that would make Marco Polo go white at the gills, of being out there all alone and expected to do it all yourself, of all those lingering close-ups of the agony and the ecstasy – it all catches up on a growing pro. The media is aware of this and uses the time-of-life crisis as part of the drama.

For years the pundits have been saying 'He went on court a boy and came off a man' of John McEnroe. They said it in 1980 when he lost to Borg, they said it in 1981 when he beat Mr Cyclops, again in 1982 when he lost to Mr Jimbo, in 1983 when he held his tongue and his service games against the Kiwi flyer, Chris Lewis. In 1984, after a startling display of opponent abuse when he defeated Jimmy Connors more hard and fast than any champion had since the days of steam radio, Malcolm Folley was one of many when he commented in the *Daily Mail* (The Paper That Supports the Czech Bully Boy of Tennis), 'In the last fortnight the spoilt, sulking kid has become a man.'

Every seasonal festivity has its distinguishing features and Wimbledon is no exception. Next year, unless he regresses to the days of his primal screaming, journalists at the front end of the paper will be inventing a sex life for the champion and putting it under a banner headline while journalists at the rear of the paper will, unless he has the surgery that once had one of Miss Navratilova's little misses on the operating table, conclude that John Patrick McEnroe has, at last, finally, definitively, become a Man.

In the old days, my elders tell me yearningly, dancing was a vertical expression of a horizontal desire. But this quaint state of affairs is, alas, no more; the unmentionable appetite has, apparently and appallingly, been assuaged in some quarters, and now many mutants would rather *dance* with the object of their affections than lie down with it. 'I'll give you a blowjob if you'll give me a dance,' a young lady tells our hero John Travolta at one point of *Saturday Night Fever*, and it is obvious that she relishes the thought of getting him on the floor much more than she relishes the thought of — excuse the expression — getting him off.

Dancing — not the Turkey Trot and the Twist, but the hip hop and the aerobic — is the newest and biggest no-sport sport of the young, utterly solipsistic and unsporting. Only one can play. The dance instinct has changed from being a desire to reach out, to merge with a complementary other to being a celebration of aloneness, of self-satisfaction, of separatism — from 'I want to screw you' to 'Screw you.' Progress!

The Dance Your Way Out Of It, Kid films have been upon us for years, starting well with *Fame* and *Fever* showing the emptiness and pathos and ambition, and declining to the depths with *Flashdance* and the breakdance abominations which play the cliché straight and shallow. In all of them an exceptionally attractive young person of thoroughly trashy yet colourful stock (roll out the clichés — blacks, Italians and Hispanics have that all-important sense of rhythm but a Jewish, Irish or Chinese hoofer has yet to tap his way out of the eternal celluloid ghetto) cuts himself a sliver of the American Dream by virtue of his flashy footwork. It says a lot about Stallone's advanced age and waistline that he was making a Boxing Film long after the Dancing Film had replaced it as the stock Hollywood potential-hood--makes-good situation.

The advantages of the Dancing as Upwardly Mobile Class Combat shtick was that both sexes could identify, and that the hero/ine could end the film as pretty as s/he started it, the greatest injury sustained being a torn leg-warmer (not even a ligament). Both these changes made the films massively attractive to the young, always the most copious cinema-goers.

The feeling behind these films, that one owes it to oneself

to hone one's body to perfection and USE it, use it as a weapon with which to fight one's way out of the mire that surrounds one, is a diluted, cordial version of a much harder, more grotesque and misthought concept that became popular in the 1980s; that as times get harder, the world gets more frightening, the only logical way to react is not to *react, resist, protest* but to turn oneself into something like steel, inviolate, indestructible. There is a new blind faith, barely admitted to, that if one eliminates enough fat and cultivates enough muscle one can bluff one's way out of absolutely anything, even perhaps − whisper it − a nuclear holocaust: avoid the big burn by going for the little burn.

Not only have homosexuals taken up bodybuilding in their search for the Ultraman (homosexuals are starting to realize that the only way they are going to get the man they want is by turning *themselves* into him), but *women*, and funniest yet *women* artists. There are few sights more hideously amusing than that of New York City artscum working out, pumping iron with the same spectacular humourlessness and miscomprehension that they bring to every other facet of their lives, never dreaming how silly the whole thing is, and how superstitious and scared their *compulsive toughening* appears to the naked eye.

The new cult of the physical, of perfect female beauty being *active* rather than passive, can be traced directly back to the Munich Olympics, the first ever invasion into the arena of female beauty by the Soviet Union when it seemed to the world that no girl had even been as beautiful as Tourischeva, as sexy as Kim, as cute as Korbut. The misses back in New York probably feel sure that they resemble these girls − living breathing perfect units of unimpeachable Soviet heroic art − as they contort their stunted little American bodies into shapes such as no man has dared venture before; but what they *really* look like are little old-fashioned functionless artists' mistresses getting into a big pigsweat over things the Russian girls have been taking for granted for twenty years now − they look like American realist art, living breathing representations of contemporary America. The mock-tough posturing shielding the played out, mouldering brain, the sad, self-obsessed, destructive search for deliverance, the grotesque monster which sees itself as supremely beautiful.

For every girl who is trying to turn herself into Charles Atlas there are, thank God, a thousand attempting to turn themselves into Jane Fonda. Aerobic dancing may be mindless and time-wasting, but then all the soulless Western girl really wants from life is a failsafe way to waste her time. It is much prettier than bodybuilding, and attracts a more pulchritudinous sort of person — the sight of Victoria Principal in a leotard is perhaps the one thing on earth capable of making a rabid atheist break down and swear that there is a God. And although there is something of a cod-supportive community shtick around some aerobics classes, the form has poignancy in that it is the definitive lonely, commercialized, competitive no-sport of the 1980s — one against one's body, mind against matter, fact against faith-healing.

The Disappearing Black

By now everyone must know the saddest story ever told: how in 1517 a Spanish Catholic priest, sickened by the abuse of the Latin American Indians, hit upon the bright idea of bringing Africans to do the New World dirty work. From Senegal to Angola the cream of numerous tribes were taken by traders, sold by their own people, and packed like cattle into slave ships, chained supine ankle to ankle below deck where more than half of them died before reaching the land of the free. There they were treated as a cross between animals and automata, put to work on the plantations of the sick South, where 'Christians' (whites) were not held legally responsible for destroying 'personal property' (slaves), where the rape of female slaves was not frowned upon but where the rape of one man's slave by another brought charges of 'damages to property', where slave births were entered into the records under 'stock', next to the animals; in the North, in the Quaker states of Pennsylvania, Connecticutt and Rhode Island, where slavery was made illegal in the eighteenth century, Negro men were weighed up as 'three fifths of a person' making their representation somewhat dubious, to say the least.

Gore Vidal once said that the Founding Fathers did not leave the Old World to escape oppression – but so they could be free to oppress others, and the story of slavery highlights hideously the foundations of cowardice and hypocrisy that the United States of America was built on. It is hardly surprising that the Americans of the South – to this day the most blood simple meatheads on this earth, outstripping even the Catholic Irish – behaved like scum-spawn, but shocking that the high-faluting, Constitution-spouting elders of the North behaved as they did. From the word go, when Thomas Jefferson removed from the Declaration of Independence his thoughts on George the Third's approval of slavery in the Colonies (of course, Britain never needed to import slaves; they had the class system) – 'He has waged cruel war on human nature itself, violating its most sacred rights of life and liberty in the persons of a distant people who never offended him' – because of pressure from the South, in order to present a united front, to the Supreme Court decision in 1896 which found in favour of a Louisiana railroad practising segregation, thus condoning the existence of a dirty little South Africaville within the United States and the springing up of those Godforsaken WHITES ONLY signs – the swastika spelt out in one syllable white trash thugspeak – like some unholy manmade flora, the North has talked like a preacher and acted like an audience at a snuff film.

The Congress, bent on keeping the shaky new land together, did not refer to slavery as such, but to 'persons held in service'. It passed a law requiring free states to return fugitive slaves to their owners. After Lincoln's election, one of the first things this giant amongst men did was to call together the elders of the free Northern blacks and tell them very nicely that their people could never live happily in the WASP's nest, and would they like a passage back to Africa? He had just the place in mind: somewhere he called 'Liberia', and never mind the fact that it already had an indigenous population – that had never stopped the USA! The few hundred that chose to take up Mr Lincoln on his kind offer of repatriation – if being thrown in the vague direction of the continent you came from can be called 'repatriation' (surely Lincoln was the Enoch Powell of the American Revolution, as populist and epic as that) – promptly got the chance to play Massah themselves; though only 4 per cent of the population, they came to rule the resident Africans – who they called 'natives' – until 1980, when power was repossessed by a group of junior officer natives.

People like to cheer Good against Evil almost as much as they like to do evil rather than good, and romantic history has it that Lincoln went to war with the South to free the slaves. The South actually fired the first shot against Fort Sumter in 1861, and seceded; they were full of themselves, rich from slave labour, ready to expand West and sick of lectures from the well-bred bluestockings of the North. One bullet did what fourteen million souls in enslavement could not do: offended Mr Lincoln. The secession from the North was the one sin that Lincoln could not tolerate; cocking a snook at the Republic, and it drove him to war.

Negroes flooded the Union camps in the South to fight for the Union; General Butler declared them 'contraband of war' and instead of letting them fight put them in camps to work for the Army. One Union officer declared slaves of the Missouri Confederates freed; Lincoln invalidated the claim. Blacks offering their services were repeatedly turned down by the Union Army, and many were returned to their Southern owners because Lincoln wanted to keep 'the Negro question' out of the war so as not to offend the border states, who kept slaves but had not seceded. In 1863, two years into the war, Lincoln signed the Emancipation Proclamation, freeing slaves in the rebel states and silently condoning the keeping of half a million slaves in the border states. Four hundred thousand blacks were now allowed to enlist in all-black regiments – paid seven dollars per month rather than thirteen. After the Union victory in 1865, the 13th Amendment was passed; 'Neither slavery nor involuntary servitude shall exist within the United States.' Slavery was officially over.

But this was a false happy ending; black comedy. Soon Lincoln was assassinated, and President Andrew Johnson pardoned the South, returned their land – which had been confiscated while the Union decided how to divide it up amongst the slaves; 'forty acres and a mule' had seemed the favourite – and granted them home rule. White home rule. In 1866 the 14th Amendment gave freed slaves the Vote, but only Tennessee ratified it, and literacy tests kept them away. In the 1850s, 97 per cent of blacks were in the South; some of the 250 revolts on record produced slaves who, after poisoning their owners or burning down their houses while they slept, escaped, and the Civil War produced more, but it was only after the phoney emancipation that

DAMAGED GODS

the migration began in earnest. The pirate element went West – 100,000 to Texas, where black cowboys became legendary (Lonesome Cowboy Old Black Joe) and to Oregon and California. In Oklahoma black towns were founded – Langston and Summit. But most went North. The industrial revolution could give them what the American Revolution had not: a job worked at for a set number of hours a day, even if it was fourteen, and a room with a door they could lock. After the savage rural South, the urban jungle they set their faces towards must have looked as beautiful as the jungles they had been taken from all those years ago.

Since before the Civil War, the free black community of the North largely revolved around the churches they had created for themselves, where they drowned their sorrows in wine, weeping and song – never had the opiate of the people appeared so potent, and been so patently useless. From the Bethel African Methodist Church of Pennsylvania to the African Methodist Episcopal Zion Church of New York City, they sang piteously about how happy they'd be when they were dead. In both North and South black colleges ground into inaction, turning out meek black teachers. The blacks might have clung for a long time to the twin pathetic pillars of respectability, religion and education, that the swaggering white trash abandoned early in favour of brute strength and amorality, if not for two things: the National Association for the Advancement of Coloured People, started by bluestockings, bluebloods and blacks in 1910, and the First World War, started by the Germans in 1914.

These fine institutions brought it home to the American blacks that brain and brawn mattered more than respectability. The European war was probably the best thing to happen to the American blacks, including Emancipation; for the first time they were allowed to show what they were made of, and they were not wanting one brain cell or biceps. The first American drafted was black; the NAACP prised from Washington the promise of a black officers' training camp if 200 black college men could be recruited – 15,000 volunteered.

To the blacks it must have seemed as though not only

Paris but France belonged to them, after what they had known in America. They were awarded Croix de Guerre and French kisses; Lieutenant Bobby Europe and his 39th Regiment Band were adored by French bobbysoxers for introducing a primal, brassy jazz to the Continent. The Americans, ever fearful and jealous of black/European rapport – the darkest and palest continents having a whale of a time together, refined, relaxed and showing America up as the bigoted, barbaric country it was – advised French girls not to fraternize with black soldiers, as it would later do in Second World War England to as little effect – party poopers are especially unwelcome during wartime, when every thrill may be the last.

In Ohio, the black scientist Garret Morgan invented the gas mask, the foremost lifesaver of WW1 Allied troops; but elsewhere Negroes moving North to work in munitions factories were terrorized by the white runts not at war. In July 1917 forty blacks were massacred in East St Louis; in 1918, returning black soldiers were lynched in their uniforms by their countrymen. In 1919 there were more than twenty-five riots as the white trash of America realized that the black population could no longer be used as an under-achieving racial ego-boost to comfort people who had nothing to boast about but the sallowness of their skins. And there were many of them, Americans being Americans; by the early 1920s, the Ku Klux Klan had four million members.

Out of the blind alleys of religion and education into the sunshine of overt shows of bravery and brainpower, which earned them even more hatred; the blacks, weary of struggle and ready for a primrose path rather than promises of pecan pie in the sky, sensed that the strongest drive of Twenties America was the desire for DIVERSION, diversion from the knowledge of the horrors that had been sprung upon blissful, ignorant America in the course of the war. By the early Twenties the Lithuanian Jew Asa Joelson was a massive star of stage, crackling 78 and in 1927 the first talking picture *The Jazz Singer*, largely due to his habit of putting on blackface and singing about his Swanee and his Mammy (or was it his Swami?) in the chilling half-human, half-jackal tones of what the boy from Sprednik fondly imagined to be the voice of the Southlands Negro minstrel. The anti-Semitism of politicized American blacks has always been hideous and obvious – from Malcolm 'X' Little using 'Jew' more constantly and derisively in his auto-biography than Hitler in his, through Jesse Jackson refer-ring to New York City as 'Hymietown' (imagine how the blacks would have gnashed their diamond-studded teeth if a Jewish leader had publicly referred to Harlem as 'Nigger-town'!) to the completely deranged Black 'Muslim' leader of today, Louis Farrakham, who said in 1984 'Hitler was an O.K. guy' – and it is not too fanciful to suggest that this prejudice might stem from some primal memory of Al Jolson capering his way to the bank in a mess of black PanStik and reassuring Whitey that though the Negro's feet may have left the plantation his soul was still there; he may have performed the world's first open heart surgery (Dr Daniel H. Williams) but he was still happiest with a song in his heart and a banjo in his hand.

They may have come to hate Mr Jolson, but they learned from him too; that blacks were most acceptable to white America when in *blackface*. The Negro adopted this protect-ive colouring in the Twenties, and ever since has gone compulsively and perversely – God knows they have little enough reason to sing and dance, or to give Whitey a cheap laugh – into entertainment, including sport. It cannot be just that opportunities to pursue other careers have not arisen: other immigrant groups in America – the Chinese, massacred from 1871 to 1885, 67 per cent of housing substandard, suicide rate three times the white average; Koreans barred from marrying whites in some states in the early part of the century; the Jews, who make up a little over 2 per cent of the American population, stopped from cultivating their massive talents by university quota systems from the Twenties to the Fifties; the Mexicans, the most decorated ethnic group of World War Two, suffering mass deportation in the Thirties; the native American Indians, killed deliberately and by the introduction of grain alcohol in their midst – the founding father Benjamin Franklin said that this would be most 'efficient' in the 'extirpation' of the 'savages' with 75 per cent unemploy-ment and life expectancy of forty-five years; the Puerto

Ricans with a lower income average than the blacks, not to mention the highest incidence in America of mental illness, drug addiction and suicide – have suffered from the inborn bigotry of the dump, yet none has gone so relentlessly and contrarily into the happy-happy business as the blacks.

Of course, none of these other groups was *forced* into America – rather, they fought to get in – and so did not have the capacity to make mainstream America feel guilty; none of them was so numerous; and none of them possessed the special sexual threat that the black man poses to the white man through no fault (*usually*) of his own. In *Birth of a Nation* D. W. Griffith portrays the Ku Klux Klan as the saviour of white Southern womanhood; and whatever they are 'saving' Miss Whitey from with reference to the Negro, it surely isn't an invitation to Lindy Hop. The WASP's lack of regard for his own sexual powers – which are, admittedly, somewhat scant – has led him to fester all kinds of fantasies, half squirming, half yearning, around the black man and his deadly weapon. It was led him to equate anti-racism on the part of white women with a burning desire for Negroid knob ('You must be a Nigger's Whore to write an article like that,' said one spiritual heir of the slick Southlands dandy of Boreham Wood and St Albans Area NF; was Rhett Butler himself ever so damnably silver-tongued? – when I suggested that burning down the houses of those of a darker hue than you might not be the best leisure activity in the world). This stubborn desire to believe that sallow sorts are itching to jump into de hay toot sweet with any toothsome black man to hand is patently a case of chronic guilt-shifting by the white man who behaved so abominably towards the black woman the first chance he got – 70 per cent of American blacks have white blood, a state of affairs stemming more from plain dirty cowardly rape than from the seductive powers or irresistible beauty of mighty Whitey, one presumes.

Whites liked blacks better when they were entertainers because of sex, guilt and numbers – over 11 per cent of Americans were black by the Twenties. Showbusiness defused the dignity of the Negro – when the Negro is dignified, no man is more so; I don't know why – and defused his sexual threat (who can take a rolling-eyed minstrel seriously as a demon lover?). It expunged guilt, too; look at them happy singing Negroes! Did six million Jews really die? Well, probably. Were twenty-eight million Africans really stolen, half of them – the lucky ones – dying in skintight transit and the survivors treated in such a way that it made cattle look like VIPs? (How many cattle were ever lynched or raped?) Hell, no – look how that there soft shoe shuffler's grinning!

They liked blacks as entertainers for many reasons, all of which helped them sleep sounder at night, and the blacks knew this and annexed entertainment as their own freedom and folly. Some went into the sporting branch of showbusiness; some into the vicious bloodsport of boxing – Negro *v.* Negro, just like the set-up fistfights on the plantation – and others went into basketball. In 1926 one Abe Sapirstein, just over five feet of British Jew, recruited five black ball players from the Chicago slums and got them games for one dollar apiece. He called them the Harlem Globetrotters to denote their tint and hint worldliness, though in fact they had never set foot in Harlem, let alone outside of America. They were soon so skilled at their sport that they ran out of opponents and started to slice their games with comedy routines – sticking the ball up their sweaters, dribbling into the stands and selling concessions. The best of black basketball talent went automatically to the Globetrotters right up till 1950, when the National Basketball Association drafted the first black player and gave the best black shots the option of playing it straight.

There is no doubt that the Harlem Globetrotters were brilliant at what they did; what they *did*, however, hardly bore inspection. Performing in front of Pope Pius XII he said to these huge men, 'My, you are a clever groups of boys!' When a wizened white celibate calls you a boy, something is rotten in the State of Vatican. Negroes fighting each other, or clowning, or playing ball, or singing or dancing or doing all the childlike, irresponsible, non-plod-jobs that make up the entertainment business, were easy to think of as boys; mischievous, lively but ultimately harmless – their crimes were more likely to be Trick or Treat than treasonous.

Certain racists like to damn the Negro with faint praise, pointing out that his talent for sports makes him 'closer to nature', more 'animal'; less human. Tosh; the reason why the American Negro is so good at sports goes back no further genetically than 1517 – the reason why the American black is such an impressive physical specimen is because unlike the other entrants to the American race, who could get into the country if they could count their fingers and spell their names, the African was chosen for his size and strongness; the quality and quantity that would make him a good slave. The cream of Africa was filtered down to the *crème de la crème d'Afrique* when half died on the slave ships; chosen genetically not once but twice, by slave trader and grim reaper, they were bound to be more physically impressive – and more frustrated when their genes did not receive their due reward. The only genetically selected group in America has also been the only one to revolt with any great force or numbers at the dirty hand that monumentally bent croupière Lady Liberty dealt them.

There is a case for calling entertainment per se evil – that's E.V.I.L., evil, simply because it diverts people so – more than any drug, and more than any love – from REAL LIFE, from the horrors being done against them/in their name. A world without institutionalized entertainment, without the great decoy, would be a world ALIVE.

When it came to the sort of showbusiness which attracts a more introverted type – the sort of entertainer who wants to *touch* rather than touch down or knock down – Negroes went into entertainment with grace and sorrow, seemingly aware that it was not the best way to spend your life or yourself – blinding other people, albeit brilliantly, to the evils of the world, especially as one of the peoples who needed the world to look *clearly* at their oppression before it could ever change. Paul Robeson, singing spirituals, presented perhaps the most perfect vision of the American Negro to this day; perfectly conscious, perfectly handsome, perfectly talented, perfectly intelligent, perfectly political.

Contrarily there was the Harlem Renaissance, when rich whites took themselves amongst poor blacks en masse – not in the cause of good works, but a good time – comporting themselves often as callously as tourists are prone to; it is hard to realize that the place where you let down your hair and bring up your dinner is a place where other people have to sweep the floors, fall in love and live. They came to hear jazz, the painted smile smeared over the gaping wound of the blues; the blues, which originated in pure sorrow, in a wordless cry developed between plantation slaves to warn each other of danger. Later these cries developed into music while you worked, songs of abduction and deliverance.

In the North, wailing blues were unacceptable because of freedom (theoretical) and tenement housing (practical). They fizzed into jazz, and the happy Negro drew his audience once more. But those who played and sang this blameless, blasé music were sad, most of them living on narcotics and memories of the South which they hated but which was home – home is where the heartache is. On his deathbed, after a lifetime of jazz, Charlie Parker asked Art Blakely, bewildered, 'when the young people would come back to playing the blues'. The writers – like Langston Hughes and Claude McKay – made only token attempts to modulate their historical sorrow; Florence Mills and Josephine Baker *did* grin and prance on Broadway, but beauty is its own justification.

The glittering blacks of the Twenties were not just good as entertainers went; of their times, they were America's finest. There was no writer of the Twenties better than Langston Hughes, or singer better than Billie Holliday, or beauty better than Josephine Baker, or human better than Paul Robeson. Sentient saints of slavery's shadows, they were painfully aware of the lurking South and its tortures; Billie Holliday was allowed to tour the South with a white band, because no one cared whether a black girl appeared outnumbered by white men – but when she toured with a black band she had to *black up* her pale brown skin lest it should seem that a suntanned white girl was consorting with black men. They knew what they were doing as they added their stitches to entertainment USA, the star-spangled blindfold, and they showed their sadness.

A little bit of the South even came to Harlem: the Cotton Club, the hottest dive, catered to whites only. And the South's worst wet dream came true as well-bred white women really did start to sleep with the dark town strutters, taking them because it was thrilling, exhilarating and forbidden, exactly as they took cocaine through other orifices.

The Thirties gave blacks two benefactors, both wealthy, powerful, cynical and slushy: Hollywood and FDR. Under Roosevelt blacks breathed deeper, forming new trades unions and using the boycott for the first time – the DON'T WORK WHERE YOU CAN'T BUY campaign, which won hundreds of jobs; Roosevelt made more than a million jobs for blacks on New Deal programmes. In 1939 Mrs Roosevelt resigned from the Daughters of the American Revolution when they blocked the black soprano Marian Anderson from singing in Constitution Hall.

Miss Anderson singing spirituals in Constitution Hall would not have been good old Negro entertainment the way Whitey liked it, but a statement of intent, and of intelligence; this is why it was not allowed. But lucking out with the WASPs mattered less when it became apparent that Hollywood was ready to clutch the black entertainer to its big, simple, sloppy, greedy kosher heart, showing once again the Jewish ability to make money out of – and *for*, which black militants find it agreeable to overlook – blacks seen from Sapirstein to Spector. In early silents Negroes were only seen as slaves; if a free, thinking Negro was called for, incredibly, a white man would black up. But in 1933 Paul Robeson appeared in Eugene O'Neill's *The Emperor Jones*, bringing his altogether Biblical beauty and strength to seven films between 1933 and 1939. The worst film of the decade, *Gone With The Wind*, showed blacks – the horrendously castrated Hattie McDaniel and Butterfly McQueen – as genial menials, but *Showboat, Imitation of Life* and *They Won't Forget* showcased white bigotry with a populist contempt unparalleled in American popular culture – or unpopular culture, come to that. What's the opposite of popular culture? – unpopular culture, which is unpopular because it's irrelevant.

Despite Roosevelt and Hollywood, from the mid-Thirties more blacks per annum left America than entered it. Perhaps they sensed that another war was on the way; and was it really worth spilling your blood for a country which

97

in peace time kept your black blood in segregated blood banks? Sure enough Japan attacked the *Arizona*, moored in Pearl Harbor, in December 1941, and a black sailor called Dorrie Miller – like all blacks in the Navy, a messman – was the first to fire back. Although more than a million blacks were drafted, the US Army and Navy remained segregated.

The Fifties were the first decade of the twentieth century; the first look at the way we live now, from deep freeze to Cold War. In the belly of beastly America, the people who had been seen, feared and not heard took their lead from the wonderful wartime propaganda America had megaphoned at the world; all that rousing, humanist Hollywood spiel about how racism was evil and men were equal. America talked too well during the war, talked so well and loud and long that even its own oppressed people – women, homosexuals, blacks – heard. Of course, when America talked of freedom it meant freedom for those oppressed by its enemies, not those oppressed by itself, but they weren't to know that. Although the Sixties are officially and rigidly the 'decade of protest' – and of course it was a very bang-bang go-go time, when political crushes replaced dance crazes – the Fifties were when the match of retaliation was put to the fuse of brutality.

You wouldn't have guessed it as you queued for your popcorn. The black slaves, saints and social problems of the Thirties cinema were refined by now to brown sugar Fun People: sexy black velvet beings who looked like panthers and sang like angels – Eartha Kitt, Harry Belafonte, Dorothy Dandridge and the aptly named Lena Horne – or Lovables like Louis Armstrong – who was popular because although he looked old enough to have practical experience of slavery never looked anything less than beatific about his place in the world – and Sammy Davis Jnr, an early practitioner of black humour: 'What's your handicap?' asked the man about to play golf with SDJ. 'I'm a one-eyed black Jew,' he replied. There were beautiful, condescending all-black films – *Porgy and Bess, Carmen Jones*, liberal Jewish Hollywood bending over backwards to show that black people could sing opera as well as anyone. When there were films in which black blood was a problem

– the remakes of *Imitation of Life* and *Showboat*, *Pinky* and *Raintree County* – white actresses played the critical roles. (Black Question as White Responsibility – Not In Front Of The Negroes.)

But off the screen, blacks were asking for more than whites could countenance. The Fifties were anything but the American Dream people pretend; they were a time of drastic postwar upheaval. The Fifties were a frightening time for whites; they saw the birth of rock and roll, 'race music' as they called it, which made the first en masse conversion – of their first born! – to what were seen as 'black' values – singing, sex, sorrow, sensation – rather than the WASPy ways of silence, chastity and optimism. The black man's music was hi-jacked and remodelled as the white kid's tantrum – can't have the keys to the car rather than can't have the keys to the leg irons. The first black judge was appointed, and the first black American – a woman – won the Pulitzer Prize. As if these weren't blows enough to Whitey's self esteem, America's sweetheart Kim Novak told her boss Harry Cohn that she was in love with Sammy Davis Jnr and intended to marry him. Cohn promptly had a heart attack, moaning, 'I wouldn't mind so much if it was Harry Belafonte!' After being informed by Cohn's mobsters that he either had to lose Miss Novak or every venue in the United States, Mr Davis quickly married a Negro dancer, Loray White.

In 1954 racial segregation was outlawed in public schools; but the South being the South, in 1957 the Governor of Little Rock, Arkansas, barred nine black teenagers from registering at the local high school, posting armed National Guard to keep them away. It took a Supreme Court verdict, a Federalized state militia AND the 101st Army Airborne Division to usher nine black teenagers into an American high school, because of the redneck anarchists of Arkansas. America, arming against the Russians, fighting against its own people.

The renewed desire of Southern blacks for education was more than the meatheads below the Mason-Dixon line could bear, being so self-consciously stupid themselves, and they stepped up their crusade of hate, hounding and homicide. It was glamour publicity to protect beautiful, intelligent Negro students entering hostile Southern universities, and postwar presidents took full advantage of the opportunities open, sending lawyers, guns and money unlimited; but it was the most banal of Everyman activities – a bus ride – which really shattered the Fifties black glass slipper.

The best thing about living in London is getting into a tube train, completely footsore and dying to sit down, realizing that all the seats are occupied by blacks and standing all across the city. Nothing is more sobering and civilizing and cheering, and nothing makes you realize more how outrageous it was that, up till 2 December 1955, Southern American blacks matter of factly gave up their seats to white passengers when buses were full. On this day one Rosa Parks refused to stand up and be discounted; three days later, after her arrest, the Montgomery Bus Boycott began, organized by the recently formed Montgomery Improvement Association, led by Dr Martin Luther King.

The first half of the American Sixties was dominated by the dreams of two men: Berry Gordy and Martin Luther King. One believed in God, the other believed in Mammon but both believed that equality was slow, sure and certain. Both dreams were magnificent, and both failed.

Berry Gordy of Detroit, Michigan, is the owner of the biggest black corporation in the world. In 1958, after trying jobs that destroyed both body and soul – boxing and the Ford assembly line – by way of making a living, the amateur song writer, who had written six local hits for his old sparring partner Jackie Wilson and been disgusted at the small royalties he received, borrowed eight hundred dollars from his family and set himself up as president of his own record label in a run-down white-brick house next door to the Sykes Hernia Control Service. By 1961 his label had a million-selling single and by 1965 forty top-twenty hits. Berry Gordy called Tamla Motown 'The Sound of Young America', a breathtakingly bold black annexation of the USA. One can only imagine the fury of a Southern redneck on hearing this tag.

Unlike the black music of the past – the blues, the gospel, the jazz, the R and B – there was nothing of the subterranean, of slavery or cellars about Motown. There was nothing historical or religious about it; it had a beautiful case of amnesia, and the people who sang it were their own heroes. It was upfront, urban and moderate, although it was far from meek – no doubt blues and gospel were blacker, but not necessarily better – they were meek, and resigned. Motown was demanding music, quick thinking, hard hitting, coming off the ropes like a born champion and confident that it had young Wayne and Wendy Whitey dancing to its tune. For the first time blacks could *really* make money out of the desperate white American desire to be diverted, *real* money, loot with roots, not just pocket money to be frittered away on hookers and heroin and hokum personal managers.

Berry Gordy *used* white musicians in a way no black brain had ever done before; the sweeping strings that lush up a hundred Motown hits were the Detroit Symphony Orchestra. Motown was emotional and excitable, as popular music always had been, but it was elegant too; the chic shall inherit the earth. If Elvis Presley sounded like Jayne Mansfield looked, blowsy and loud and low, Motown was Audrey Hepburn. It was fresh and whole-some and *never* overtly sexy. If Presley had converted white youngsters to what were thought to be black values like promiscuity and pessimism with his early, wailing work about cheap women, heartbroken men, seedy hotels and blue suede shoes, Tamla Motown preached a toe-tapping creed of chastity and optimism, of hunger and fun hot on the trail of a place in the sun. Sad or happy, loving or losing, early Motown was about boys and girls rather than men and women; not so much a righting of wrongs as a whiting of wrongs.

Later, in songs like 'Love Child', 'Poppa Was A Rolling Stone', 'Ball Of Confusion' and 'Simple Games', morals and problems came fuzzily into focus, and personal con-servation mixed with political liberalism were thrust at the confused dancer. But in the early King Kennedy Sixties optimism was as natural as breathing and fingers popped, not wagged. It didn't matter what the motivation behind the music was; Tamla Motown, from the early Sixties to the mid Seventies, was *the* perfect moment, the apex of culture

– black or white, ancient or modern. If ever there was a justification for the abduction of the Africans, Tamla Motown was it. Like the pyramids, the overwhelming beauty of Motown music obliterates the evil that made its existence possible. Motown could not have happened without slavery, though; a hard knowledge.

As a corporation it was *so* successful simply because no one had ever assembled so much sheer talent in one place before; it made MGM – 'More Stars Than There Are In The Heavens' – look like a flophouse. Songs that would become as much a part of people's lives as their living, breathing friends were written in one part of the building while in the Artists Development Department some raw young ghetto girl would be being taught how to smoke a cigarette with eclat. They were taught how to speak, how to save their money to their best advantage, how to pay tax and how to climb decently out of a limousine in a sequinned sheath second skin (the girls too).

The contenders and pretenders of Motown resented Berry Gordy's punitive paternalism and diehard favouritism, and by the late Sixties, when Motown's grip was loosening, they drifted away – usually never to be heard of again. Berry Gordy didn't care – he had built the perfect beast, Diana Ross, and in 1971 he moved Motown to Los Angeles so that she could pursue her film career. The dream was for Ross to play Billie Holliday, a piece of casting that made Hollywood and hipsters alike snigger; eventually financing the film itself, *Lady Sings The Blues* earned Gordy twenty million dollars, earned Diana Ross an Oscar nomination and both of them tremendous respect. The casting, miraculously, was perfect; this girl, the ultimate black winner who was so successful that the hip decreed she was not black at all, as this other girl, who lost and wept and wailed her way through life and thus was reckoned to be blacker than anyone. There was no credibility gap in the way Ross portrayed her; the old inverted snobbery which had measured blackness in buckets of tears was officially over.

Perhaps part of Berry Gordy's desire for Diana Ross to play Billie Holliday – a promiscuous, lachrymose heroin addict, hardly the sort of role you'd think he'd choose for his most treasured, pampered, personally managed possession – was ominous. Perhaps he had wanted to show her what happened to black girl singers who tried to go it alone without a clever man with a megaplan behind them. It didn't work; the film was still in the cinemas when she married a white public relations man (they divorced in 1976) and in 1981 she left Motown for RCA and around seven million pounds. Berry Gordy, not a ball of fiery emotion, for the first time expressed anger and confusion at the defection of an artist. Like some black billionaire Okie he had picked up his property and headed West to make a future for himself and the woman he loved, and like a bitch she had left him high and dry in the Hollywood Hills. The guts – Detroit – had been torn out of the Motown machine in 1971, and the heart – Ross – ten years later. But the shell remained the same.

Lionel Richie is now Motown's top artist, and though he makes Mr Gordy a lot of money it is dubious whether he makes the million-dollar heart beat a little faster. Lionel Richie has no sex appeal and nothing to say, except I LOVE YOU, DARLING, endlessly. Thanks to him, Motown doesn't call females women; now it calls them ladies. The ladies who make up at least 80 per cent of Mr Richie's audience are white and affluent, and thanks to them he has become a multi-millionaire in the five years since he left the funky, chunky Commodores for paler pastures. His invariably slow songs are not offensive, but they are profoundly dull, and looking at that Motown label in the middle there is like looking at the desecration of a religious icon – the last blasphemy of the Godless generation. Motown does not sound young any more, or profound, or perfect as it did; it is a monolith – stereolith? – and just another record label, not the sound of the cream of a people in motion at last. 'It sells or it smells', the brash young Berry Gordy was fond of saying when he loved his monster so much that a dropped aitch or a dropped arch worried him as much as a dropped sale. Now, as the head – not the heart or the soul any more, just the head – of a company – not a crusade or a miracle any more, just a company – which has occasion to celebrate if it gets a single which is not by Lionel Richie in the Top Fifty, Berry Gordy must know that the

Motown pong has never been so strong.

Martin Luther King, whose bus boycotts became a popular leisure activity in the late Fifties, was a believer in the strange methods of the famous Indian Mr Gandhi, who believed – or said he did – that non-violent civil disobedience was the most powerful weapon against oppression. Obviously he had gone out in the midday sun without his parasol once too often.

The importance of Mr Gandhi has been greatly exaggerated since his death, to the extent that he is believed in some quarters to have won India its independence. This claim is as easily understood as it is dismissed; of *course* it is to the advantage of the white world in general and the colonialists in particular to show Mr Gandhi in a powerful and effective light. When peoples rise up and rebel against those who have misappropriated their land, it is nice to be able to point back at history and say, 'Look at Mr Gandhi, though! *He* just sat crosslegged in a sheet when he didn't like the way India was going, and *he* got what he wanted!' Of course those in power would prefer their opponents to wind themselves up in a sheet and sit down rather than run at them brandishing a pickaxe handle – who wouldn't? But the fact remains that in the spring of 1947, communal violence in India reached a peak, leading Viceroy Mountbatten to recommend an early independence in pursuit of calm. The Indian Independence Act was law by the summer. Violence gave India back to the Indians; the faceless, benign god violence.

Non-violent protest got the Southern Negroes a chance to take the weight off their feet, as black and white together sat down at segregated lunch counters, department stores and libraries all through the South in 1960, but not much else. No doubt they were brave; but no one was going to shoot an unarmed civilian for sitting down plain and simple, not even in the South, especially not in the global village. When they tried for more by non-violent means – the Freedom Rides of 1961, when two buses full of integrated passengers drove from Washington DC to New Orleans as a protest against the still prevalent segregation of public transport in the South (a fat lot of good the Fifties boycotts had done in the long run) – all they got was arrested (four hundred of them) or dead (three).

Martin Luther King would have made a good leader for the Flat Earthers – who realized that their case was a little, uh, *unreasonable*, and that there was a lot of slow, solid spade(sic)work to be done before the people at large realized their folly and joyously admitted that yes, the world *was* flat – but for the most consistently sinned against people in the Western world he was not Mr Right. Beautiful, spiritual, beloved of the rich and famous, his weakness was that which blacks have always seen as their strength, and which has always effectively neutered them: religion. His faith made him too patient, and his pacifism made him maddening to bitter urban blacks – nobody's flock, who would rather have been washed in the blood of the pig on the beat than the lamb in the Bible.

Martin Luther King asked too much of the blacks and delivered too little. In 1963 Negroes still found it in themselves to march in over eight hundred peaceful protests in support of President Kennedy's ever so modest proposed civil rights legislation, peaceful despite the dogs and water cannons of the police. In a Negro Christian Church in Alabama, four tiny black girls were killed by a white bomb, and still Mr King drivelled on about God and patience. Although he was not assassinated until 1968, he reached his most eloquent, impotent peak on 28 August 1963 when 250,000 people assembled in Washington DC to hear him speak at the Lincoln Memorial.

The idea of a black march on Washington had been the idea of A. Philip Randolph of the Brotherhood of Sleeping Car Porters – not a church, but a trade union – though it had just floated around for some twenty years. But three years into Kennedy's presidency, with voting still out of bounds to Southern blacks due to literacy tests, there was pressure within the nationwide black communities to lean on Mr Wonderful a little; march on Washington and lie down on the streets and airport runways. (It is odd how when American blacks stand up for their rights this always involves sitting or lying down.) When rumours of this reached the White House, the Administration quickly insisted that it 'approved' and 'welcomed' this before whisking six civil rights leaders off to New York City, donating eight hundred thousand dollars through a philanthropic agency and promising another similar sum if the march went 'well'. By well, it did not mean 'effective' so much as 'quiet'.

Chartered planes flew in movie stars that day, and marchers were asked not to bring banners – banners would be provided. The huge crowd had been told to sing just one song; 'We Shall Overcome'. *'We shall overcome . . . some day'*, the crowd sang beautifully – some day indeed. One English newspaper described the march as 'a gentle flood', which meant it was useless. At the Lincoln Memorial, where that kind Mrs Roosevelt had arranged for Marian Anderson to sing after the DAR had blocked her from Constitution Hall in 1939, that kind Mr Kennedy had arranged for Martin Luther King to speak. Like the spirituals of Miss Anderson Mr King's speech was immaculately beautiful, full of the suffering and stolidity of American Negro history. It was also as politically relevant to the twentieth century. The call and response harmonies of the speech, the perfectly modulated voice of Mr King, the toning banners and the order of the masses; it could have been choreographed and scored by Berry Gordy, and it passed out of the public consciousness the way a hit record drops out of the charts when its moment has gone. In a press poll that summer, not one Congressman or Senator with a record of opposition to civil rights said that he had changed his views; on the contrary, the redneck being what he is it is likely that this great show of patient pacifism merely increased his contempt for the Negro. Patience is not the way of America, but rather smash, grab and gloat. For a Negro leader to talk of having 'dreams' which would overcome 'some day' was a wonderful sop to the South and a terrible insult to the people he was supposed to be leading.

When King died he was in the process of organizing another march on the capital, part of a 'Poor People's Campaign' that asked why the disadvantaged of all races were being ignored. (Thirteen years of Dr Gandhi's Patent Faith Healing Medicine had obviously not proved the miracle cure he had hoped it would be.) Though only in his forties, he had lived a long time for a maverick black leader, perhaps because he asked for so little so slowly.

Malcolm 'X' Little died three years before King, killed by a former brother Black Muslim, dying a vendetta gangster's death. It was suitable; he had always lived like a gangster, after all, even after going to jail for petty crime, finding God in a blind Allah, and coming out in 1952 to live off his fast hustler's mouth, prostituting black liberation rhetoric as he had once prostituted black women before his conversion. Celebrated by the deliciously appalled white media, shunned by the black community, he was bad news from the moment of his unfortunate birth; a rogue male, mad, crazy, from a family with a history of insanity, bellowing and stamping insistently towards the moment of violent death.

The Black Muslims, a sect peculiar – in more ways than one – to America, were founded in 1929 when one Elijah Poole saw Allah on the street (very likely). If the breath-alyser had existed in those days, perhaps Mr Poole might have pulled himself together, had a nice lie down and gone about his business; but it didn't, and as others saw pink elephants, he saw black Allahs. Because blacks are always on the lookout for a new religion in which to drown their sorrows, he made converts, including the prime catch of dope dealer and addict, burglar and pimp Malcolm Little who got religion in jail as dull, weak characters are liable to.

For the profoundly ignorant and superstitious black petty criminal, Black Islam was perfection itself. Like the rednecks who are their mirror image, Black Muslims are peasants of the worst kind, revelling in their prejudices, senseless mysticism and half-remembered childhood warnings about de Devil who will come and get you ass if you bad. Like all half-assed voodoo masquerading as serious political creed, it places great importance on sexual conduct; in fact the Black Muslims' obsessively, neurotic-ally masculine views on homosexuality, the rights of women and interracial sex and marriage line up *exactly* with those of the Moral Majority. (They both believe in segreg-ation, too. In short they are a Reaganite's wet dream; won't touch your real estate, won't touch your women and they'll help you fire-bomb the family planning clinics, too.)

In theory, at least. In 1963 Malcolm 'X' was dismissed from the Black Muslims after voicing his displeasure with the conduct of his revered leader, Elijah Poole, who despite his teachings against adultery and fornication transpired to have been engaged in adulterous fornication with a procession of secretaries who now presented him with paternity suits. Instead of congratulating the sixty-seven-year-old holy man on his stamina, Malcolm reacted like a jilted bride, and on the rebound formed the Organization of Afro-American Unity. Sadly, although the name spanned two continents, the membership barely spanned two seats. Consumed with self-hatred – red-haired, he was about as black as Rita Hayworth – his targets were the things that had made him – interracial sex – the things he had been – drug dealers, black men who slept with white women – and the things he envied – educated blacks, integrated blacks, Jews, whites. He called non-blacks, 'the white devil', conveniently ignoring the fact that since 1859, when the white Virginian John Brown had led a posse of forty-four white men and five blacks on the arsenal at Harper's Ferry to get arms to lead a slave insurrection and been hung for his trouble to 1965, when a white housewife giving a lift to a black demonstrator down in Selma, Alabama, for the civil rights march was shot by the Ku Klux Klan, hundreds of whites have put their lives on the line for blacks. Maestro of the manifesto, it is doubtful that Malcolm X ever flexed any part of his body in service of the black community except his jawbone. Or his wrist bone, as he took his money for the dope he had sold them.

A very common white trash personality type – petty criminal with insanity in family goes to jail, gets religion and messianic delusions – only Malcolm X's pigmentation got him publicity. He got it from masochistic Jewish journalists who felt guilty about passing for white; blacks knew bad news when they heard it, and avoided him. Alex Haley, who helped X translate his monumentally confused thoughts into something approximating Humanoid in aid of his 1964 autobiography, admits that in Sixties Harlem, on bar stools and stoops, people were saying that all X did was TALK. (What else did they expect the most celebrated

talking head of the day to do?) 'All he's *ever* done was talk
. . . some of those people of Dr King's are out getting beat
over the head.' Angry rhetoric could blind guilty Whitey to
inaction, but the blacks knew a chicken when they saw one.

X was very irked when a 1964 *New York Times* poll of
Negroes showed that three fifths considered Mr King to be
doing 'the best work for Negroes', another one fifth rated
Roy Wilkins of the NAACP while only 6 per cent voted for
him. Polls, and press, and autobiographies – it says a lot
about the incredibly media-orientated, sedentary career of
X that he found time in 1964 to write his autobiography –
these were the trophies that Malcolm X secretly coveted.
(And a home in the suburbs; just before he was killed he put
down a down payment on a house in very Jewish Long
Island. Obviously 'the sickness of integration' had got to
him.) More than anything else he liked to point a quivering
finger at blacks who colluded with whites to give them
'thrills' – sexual, political – but he gave whites more
delicious shivers down the spine than all the other black
voices put together. Coming along at a time when the white
media was scared that all blacks were as intelligent and
reasonable as Dr King, Malcolm X was the perfect mad dog
proof of black Otherness. He was living, seething proof
that blacks weren't like whites; the boogieman in the three
piece suit, the white devil drag.

Not so much a freedom fighter as a frisson, Malcolm X
never raised a hand to help his people. He was the paper
tiger to King's lamb/lion, the psycho to King's saint, but he
was above all else a cheap thrill. He thrilled in death as he
had thrilled in life; 'I'm here to mourn a fascinating man,'
said a young white woman to a TV reporter. Fascinating;
not important, or wonderful, or brave, but *fascinating*, like a
reptile you watch through glass and perhaps write a thesis
about. Fascinating. X may have changed his name, but was
Little all his life.

He had the talk and no action; King had the action (albeit
unarmed and ultimately ineffectual) but talked as though
calming a fractious baby rather than 11 per cent of the
American people. Hush hush . . . one day, one day . . .

But by 1966 the finest ever expression of black anger –
mouth and motion – was making a fist. If I've only one life,

let me live it as a blonde, went a popular advertising slogan of the Sixties. The American Negro now saw a variation on the theme. If I've only one life, let me live it as a BLACK.

When it came to fighting back, Negroes had always preferred to praise the Lord rather than pass the ammunition. But by 1965 they had lost their fear of God and guns. Decent Christian black men had boycotted, marched, sat-in, lain down, tap-danced and tried every other means of peaceful protest against persecution for the past decade to no visible effect – only 14 per cent of all black Southern children attended desegragated schools. Mr King had gone like some latterday Mr Smith to Washington asking the American people to make good the promise of the American Dream; perhaps he hadn't noticed that Jimmy Stewart was white. The tragedy of King was that he was the archetype American innocent abroad in a foreign country; his vision of the United States was that of liberal Hollywood, with good winning out over evil and love proving stronger than hate. He may as well have taken his hunger marches down the yellow brick road with Dorothy and Toto to make up the numbers.

Another factor was Vietnam. For the first time the pacifism King urged on blacks – that 28 per cent of combat troops were black already, and that they should not go – was to their good; the first time he had not advocated mindless non-violence. When Muhammad Ali, the most physically revered black man of the twentieth century, announced his decision to go to jail rather than Vietnam, pacifism developed muscles, and it began to look more machismo to resist the war rather than go along with it. There was only so much black pacifism to go around; when blacks practised it against the Viet Cong, they had to withdraw it from America, who had had it for a long time. Too long.

In early 1965 whips and tear gas were used against King's ever-patient peaceful protesters in Selma, Alabama; by mid-August a massive riot in the black Los Angeles district of Watts had killed thirty-five people and caused one hundred million pounds worth of damage. Over the next three years black riots came with the summer, like forest fires choreographed by the celestial Malcolm X, spreading from ghetto to ghetto all over America. The struggle had stopped being about civil rights and was now about civil war; war in fits and starts, with phoney truces and scattered troops, but war nevertheless. Black patience, personified by King, had had its day and black pride took the steering wheel.

Unorganized black pride used fire, burning down the homes that their ancestors had escaped to from the South and slavery – the Promised Ghetto – which had now become cages (the only burning down blacks would be doing in the Eighties would be setting fire to a line of cocaine in order to freebase, but let us not think of that right now). Then they were hot; and everything they touched turned to righteous fire.

But organized blacks used firearms, to far greater effect. In 1966 the Black Panther Party for Self Defence evolved from the rhetoric of the SNCC's violent virtuoso Stokely Carmichael, the Tom Jones of the black struggle who would later marry Miriam Makeba and go the whole hearts and flowers, robes and bones through noses African drag route. The BPPSD was built from loving scratch and broken camel's back by Huey Newton, a law student, and Bobby Seale, an Air Force veteran, street tough and general nogoodnik, who felt that Mr Carmichael's highly photogenic anger had more to do with his exclusion from the double-garaged white horn of Cornucopia than his revulsion at capitalist-imperialism per se. Carmichael was a separatist who wanted plush ethnic ghettos furnished by a black economy and culture, a defeatist; he invented the slogan 'Black Power', which really meant black buying power – the *Ebony* tower. The Black Panthers tried to sum up their ambitions in a manifesto you could get on the back of a matchbox – 'Power to the People!' But then it is always difficult to express big dreams without sounding simpleminded. If someone came up to you in the street and told you he was dedicated to life, liberty and the pursuit of happiness, you would call for a policeman.

The Panthers were the first black dissenters not made peasants by religion (Martin Luther King), separatism (Carmichael) or both (Little X). They didn't waste time wearing out what little shoe leather the black community had tramping them back and forth between ghetto and seat of government acquiring yet more useless pieces of legislation to paper their prison cells with. Despite their street demon drag – the leather jacket of the thug, the beret of the Resistance, the highly polished shoes of the pimp and the dark sunglasses of the psychopath – the early works of the Black Panthers verged on the saintly – or at least on what any *decent* country would have done for its underprivileged as a matter of course. They had traffic lights put up at accident black spots, fed the hungry, tested for sickle cell anaemia and policed the brutal Oakland police force from a car containing a gun and a law book. Huey and Bobby might have been more like Beveridge and Bevan than Bonnie and Clyde if America had been more like Britain. But America is America, and never more nakedly than through the murderous medium of its police force; a savage continent whose leaders pass for civilized, for *normal*, only by benefit of their pasty faces.

In the cock-conscious Eighties the Panthers' insistence on combining good works with loaded guns – rifles and pistols hung from them as polished and proud as medallions from a ghetto procurer – smacks of machomania; but the police of Oakland were armed and extremely dangerous. It was self-defence – and you may as well be hung for a shotgun as a Luger. White America had always got a cheap laugh from the screen face of a terrified black – the big bulging eyes, quivering rubber lips and shaking knees never failed to hit the spot. Now the woebegone worm had turned, and the brand new black bravado made beautiful, bone-chilling pictures; the perfect six o'clock news trailer of the horror movie coming shortly to your white neighbourhood. Who was laughing now?

(Tom Wolfe for one. He saw in the patronage of the Panthers by rich East Coast glitterati the stuff of classic drawing-room comedy of errors. It was Wolfe – speaking as much from a *racial* perspective as the Panthers did; sons of the South, Virginia in his case, had *always* chided the Northern Negro-befrienders (especially if they happened to be new Hebrew money, like Leonard Bernstein) for not *understanding* the Negro, for talking to him as an *equal* and *upsetting* him – who coined that cute, utterly meaningless

112

sneer-made-speech 'radical chic' to dismiss as silly and superficial those rich whites who had the decency to feel a little racial guilt and the temerity to try and help a just cause when they came across one.

(Reading *Radical Chic*, one gets the impression that Mr Wolfe likes his rich whites the way rich whites have always liked their blacks; give them a warm toilet, a tight pussy and a slab of watermelon and they'll be happy. Except for Mr Bernstein and his bleeding heart friends substitute a warm jacuzzi, a tight pair of designer jeans and a line of good coke.)

But no one else found the Panthers funny. Their strutting and bravado, though it came from the exalted worthless of the ghetto, the pimps and the pushers, was a necessary weapon against police intimidation; a loaded gun was the only language the LAPD understood. The first time Huey Newton showed an Oakland policeman his shotgun and said, 'Don't you know that by the Fourteenth Amendment of the US Constitution that you can't remove a person's property from them without due process of law?', the policeman rushed back to his car and screamed into the radio, 'They got guns. They got guns. They got guns. Niggers down here got guns. Get me some help down here. Niggers got guns, they got guns.' Niggers got guns; the ultimate American Nightmare. Of course it had always been a Negro's right to bear arms, as it was every other adult American's. But now, for the first time, the guns were being maintained with some higher ideal in mind than turning over the liquor store cashbox next Saturday night. In a land where gun love ranks even higher than mother love the sight of black knights in shiny leather armour caressing the cold steel that America was built on must have seemed as obscene and incredible to the police as a Panther fondling some white policeman's grey-haired old Mom.

It was not surprising that the Panthers attracted a considerable number of rich, pretty, white women – Jane Fonda, Jean Seberg, Elizabeth Taylor – in every capacity from bedwarmer to bankroller, and often both. The Panthers were, after all, the end product of a double-sorting process enacted upon the biggest and best men in

Africa, and handsome in any context – on a catwalk or a Vistavision screen they would still have looked extraordinary. When you put them against the backdrop – all straggling facial hair and rank fatigues – of student-based West Coast protest, they were irresistible: Maoists with muscles. To rebellious WASPy princesses, black and red was the best possible colour combination.

And the Panthers were in the American tradition; the outnumbered, true-hearted outlaw who stares and shoots down the corrupt opposition crushing the poor but honest (well, petty criminal) community by reign of terror, and with the aid of his trusty pistol taking what is truly his (including the beautiful schoolteacher, played by Angela Davis). These screen angels had grown up in the John Wayne Fifties; they had been bred by America to worship men like the Black Panthers.

Unlike the black separatists the Panthers were not so sexually precarious that they felt they were being 'used' by the white women they associated with (no more so than is inevitable, anyway; sex without using is as difficult as eating without chewing, from both angles) – Huey Newton was even seen *holding the door* open for a white woman. The Sixties were the worst decade in history for feminist considerations on the part of men – there were even more important things to do, such as the supremely vital act of running a pig for the Democratic nomination as the Yippies did in Chicago in 1968 – and if brilliantly educated white upper-middle (upper *muddle*) graduates thought of Betty Friedan only when they wanted to stop themselves from coming, it was a bit rich expecting the black, unmanned since the birth of the US, to tread lightly lest he strut over the sensitive toes of feminism. In 1969 Bobby Seale drew attention sternly to the fact that 'brothers' were accusing 'sisters' of being 'counter-revolutionary' if they refused to put out; this had long been the practice amongst the well-educated white student disciples of the armed dance crazes, with no official condemnation by their leaders whatsoever. Like the men, Black Panther women were instructed to familiarize themselves with the works of Mao and the workings of firearms; and there was certainly no white girl equivalent of Angela Davis.

Probably the most objectionable thing about the Panthers was their language; they could not say 'The cat sat on the mat' without interjecting the word 'muthafucka' at least twenty-five times. But as it took a black boxer to make black pacifism respectable, virile, the Black Panthers probably reckoned that it would take profanity to make the thoughts of Lenin easy listening to the street-calloused blacks they needed to educate and recruit to boost their numbers – by 1968 they had only 3000 members, even though J. Edgar Hoover was calling them 'the greatest threat to the internal security of this country'.

The founding fathers of the Black Panther Party had one fatal flaw, a white man's weakness: they believed that criminals were victims of society. Where the civil rights movement called upon blacks young and old, respectable and rebellious, the Panthers concentrated on enrolling the black community's criminal element. All the robbers, rapists, pimps and pushers lured into the Party would be miraculously transformed into good loyal servants of the people they had harrassed and harmed ('I started out practising on black girls in the ghetto,' wrote Eldridge Cleaver of his career of rape, in a statement whose racism – black girls as something to 'practise' on before perfecting one's art on the real thing, white women – was worthy of the Ku Klux Klan) once they had undergone the baptism of political consciousness-raising; just say three Hail Maos and your sins would be forgiven.

As time passed and publicity increased it became clear that the Panthers were confusing self-defence and self-promotion. Like so many rebels of the day they had become intoxicated by their own press releases; some of them actually enjoyed posing with pistols for film star photo-journalists more than bringing home the bacon to the ghetto and making breakfast for schoolchildren. When Newton and Seale were in jail Eldridge Cleaver took over, and he more than anyone was addicted to violence; he was the bad seed who saw black pride as some sort of ethnic aftershave – splash it all over and feel like a new, big man. Less and less time was spent on the Panthers' original reformist Ten Point Programme, which reflected the immediate needs of the community – housing, employment, medicine – and more on provoking shoot-outs with the police.

They started out as violent, virtuous visionaries and ended up as dead social workers, fitting shoes for the shoeless in the morning and getting blown away by the police at night. From 1967 to 1970, Black Panthers were cornered and killed by police in New York, New Haven, Washington, Detroit, Oakland, Chicago and Los Angeles. Because they were armed, it was easy for police to claim they had killed them in self-defence; the pacifism of Martin Luther King's people had been seen as the ultimate bravery, but the Panthers were much braver to go armed into confrontation.

The best were jailed, the second best were dead and the worst – Mr Cleaver – fled to Algeria. The rest decided that death was too high a price to pay for Panther glamour, so when the going got tough the toughs got going – as far away from the Panthers as possible. Looking for a new hero, they found Shaft.

Shaft was black pride without the politics; which came out as black swagger. His style, from leather coat to street sus and sass, was pure Panther, but he was the Panther who came in from the cold, put down his Fanon and picked up his *Ebony*. He was still fighting for the black community; but this time round, the only oppressors of the black community were black gangsters. Shaft's blackness was really nothing more than protective colouring; like the slattees of the African coast, he worked for white men.

But no one ever called him Uncle Tom, because he came on like a black Superman, albeit with a permanent hard on (for when Shaft wasn't out making the streets safe for decent black folk to be exploited in he was making some beautiful Angela Davis lookalike). Not so much Steppin Fetchitt as Steppin Shootitt.

How different was Shaft from the last big screen black detective, Virgil Tibbs, who had been closer to Sherlock Holmes than Marvin Hagler. As played by the beautiful Sidney Poitier, Virgil Tibbs was a man of science and an expert in forensic deduction who didn't use his fist much but nevertheless insisted on being called *Mr* Tibbs. No one ever called Shaft *Mr* Shaft.

It is common, conman knowledge that Shaft was a black man's hero and Sidney Poitier a white liberal's wet dream; I am not so sure of this, and think that Sidney Poitier was far and away the most subversive and Whitey-frightening black screen presence there has ever been. Two minutes of *Guess Who's Coming To Dinner?* deal more blows to the soft racist underbelly than a whole two hours of *Shaft, Shaft In Africa, Carry On Shaft* and whatever came next; unless you believe that a black man's integrity can be measured by the size of his Afro.

Entering films at twenty-six in 1950, Sidney Poitier was immediately the first black man to be an international lust object. When you look at Sidney Poitier, you see SEX; he is so beautiful he makes you want to weep, like Marilyn Monroe did – some sort of epic evolution. As terminally masculine as she was feminine – often to his disadvantage, for when many dumb pundits see a beautiful face they also automatically see a stupid and unconscious one – he could be anything: sexy, funny, tense, boring, yet always compulsive. He was as talented, as tender, as intelligent and as easily laughed off by those who should have been proudest of him.

In the Seventies and Eighties, blacks from Richard Roundtree to Eddie Murphy would play pimps, pugilists, policemen, petty criminals and crooners with room temperature IQs, and in some way be taken as contributing to black 'identity' and 'pride'. Sidney Poitier, playing men of science, of academia, of action (although he did play his share of convicts and cause célèbre rebels, too; people like to overlook this, as it makes the simple-minded label of 'Uncle Tom' a little blurred and smudgy), was somehow perceived as a sell-out. In order to be a 'real' black, it sometimes seemed, one had to take the jobs that real racists believe blacks belong in and are best suited to: the pimping, grinning, gunning, running scared ghetto jobs of crime and punishment. Blacks living in ghettos, policing in them or pimping in them or pushing in them or entertaining in them are perfectly acceptable in white racist societies – you'll even find them in South Africa.

Sidney Poitier is a *professional* man, with a high income and great expectations. While the Shafts and Superflies and

Beverley Hills Cops stay away from *white jobs* and *white women*, albeit with the maximum of bratty braggadocio, Sidney Poitier, very politely, takes them both. In the nicest possible way – *Mr* Poitier is never less than a gentleman – he sees no reason why he should not have what the white man refers to as OUR jobs and OUR women. He will not settle for being Kingshit of the ghetto; he will settle only for what he *wants*, and if Whitey thinks that *thing* – that girl, that des. res., that situation vacant – is by some divine right his . . . *tough*.

In 1967 he made two films – *Guess Who's Coming To Dinner?* and *To Sir With Love* – in which he ends up engaged to be married to a brace of beautiful respectable white schoolteachers, whose love and admiration he retains even after they have been pressured to disengage themselves from him. The idea that a beautiful, respectable white schoolteacher would *marry* a black man – as if *sleeping* with one wasn't bad enough – was the most direct blow to the cold heart of white supremism possible. As Mr Poitier sets off into two different sunsets with frail, aristocratic Katharine Houghton and Suzy Kendall – surely the very sort of well-bred white sylph who the missionaries had warned would be ACTUALLY, PHYSICALLY INJURED by congress with a black man – to bed down with God's blessing, move into a white neighbourhood and raise cute coffee-coloured kinder, he is that creature most feared and hated by every bigot from George Wallace to Malcolm X; the black man who has beaten the white man at his own game.

From Poitier and the Panthers it was a long slide downhill into sitting pretty in Whitey's lap. Poitier/ Panthers tried to show that a black man could come out of the ghetto and still be someone that counted, someone to be proud of; but somewhere in the Seventies, after the retirement of one and the destruction of the other, the pride was watered down into a vain, narcissistic strut, and blacks went back, in spirit if not in zip code, to the ghetto and its small pecking order (pecker order? – black self-esteem became once more very dependent on being thought to be a sex machine). Narcissism, garish and gullible, was the only brand of pride a black man was free to cultivate without the

118

implicit threat of liquidation à la Panther mode.

Not strong enough to regroup and repeatedly go for that of white America's which they wanted, blacks were far from being the only dissenting Americans to call a retreat. When the Children's Revolution of the Sixties did not come off as choreographed and the grown-ups were re-elected in the gruesome shape of President Nixon, the students gave up like babies building a toppled brick tower. The Seventies ideas of controlling one's OWN destiny, SELF-discovery, SELF-awareness and PERSONAL growth all arose from feelings of defeatism and powerlessness, from a conviction – as strongly held as revolution had once been – that one could not affect the change of anything beyond the state of one's complexion or the curl of one's hair. Social conscious-ness shrunk on a wide scale to nothing more hopeful than calorie consciousness.

Many blacks could never buy the politics of the Panthers or the ambitions of Poitier; power and position, political or personal, bring with them responsibility, and the black community just as much as the white working class nurse chronic doubt in their own capabilities. The move from communal struggle to personal survival – *survival* was *the* big buzzword of the Seventies, usually used to disguise an individual's greedy and selfish behaviour; it implied that the world was a jungle, and justified your cut-throat tendencies – and the retreat into the *Ebony* tower came as something of a relief to blacks, allowing them to take the cerebral weight off their feet. Segregation could not be dealt with in a day, but bad breath could. The blacks needed to *win*, even if the battle was against nothing bigger than their own body odours.

From the South Bronx to Mad Ave, this conditioner surrender was good news. The black separatists had often dreamed of economic segregation – black money going into black business. But the black man's economic segregation became the white man's market segmentation, and con-sumer goods from Hollywood to hair gel (it is small wonder that blacks have little time for armed insurrection, what with all the *Ebony* advertisements tell them they have to do to their hair to stop it from being – God forbid! – too dry/kinky/limp/frizzy) followed. 'Black is beautiful', as said by

Marcus Garvey, was originally a statement of Afro-Caribbean pride and solidarity; in the Seventies it wound up as the best way to sell an Afro wig.

The Seventies were not all bad for blacks; they started with the welcome death of Jimi Hendrix, every hippie's favourite black and a true Uncle Tom, who had forsaken everything blacks had been proud of from sharp suits to sweet soul music to dress like a white hippie slob, taken the drugs of a white hippie slob, play the tuneless, masturbatory guitar of a white hippie slob and died the messy death of a white hippie slob – choking to death on his own vomit while sleeping after taking too many tranquillizers. He was the hideous hybrid of Uncle Tom and Noble Savage, those great white enthusiasms, and when he died the job went to the Jamaican singer Bob Marley, possibly the most stupid, duplicit black man since Malcolm X. Marley sang about going back to Africa (and moved to Miami, Florida, playground of the rich and the retired Jewish – like Little X's Long Island). He sang about standing up for one's rights (and constantly smoked and advocated the brain-tranquillizer marijuana). He sang about the salt of the earth African woman (and slept with Miss World). He was the black Rod Stewart, right down to his passion for football and his conviction – despite what Galileo may have said – that the world revolved around his cock. If you ever needed to know just how badly the black will to fight for their rights on earth had been atrophied by centuries of stewing in religion and opiates – promises of dope today, jam tomorrow and life after death – you had only to listen to Bob Marley records – with their endless refrains of 'Everything's gonna be all right' (even more of a don't-hold-your-breath lullaby than 'We shall overcome . . . SOME day') – for everything to become depressingly clear.

When Marley died in 1981 his Uncle Savage mantle passed to the cutely named Nigerian entertainer Fela Kuti, who shared a similar ability to make almost unbelievably tedious music (there can be no doubt that pure black music is as deadly dull as pure white music; this is why repeated left-field attempts to launch African music onto the public consciousness have proved as futile as would attempts to relaunch the music of, say, Marie Lloyd – not because of state racism, but because of a low boredom threshold and because pure is a bore) and a similar sick attitude towards women: basically that they are just walking holes, baby machines. The white hipster is still so hung up on the dirty fears the racists peddled – and that he bought, against his better judgement – concerning the black man's natural, superior sexuality that he cannot recognize the terrible superstitious dread the African has of sexwomen – the white hipster would prefer to see it as 'black culture', 'tradition', and therefore sacrosanct. Thus the white missionaries who pleaded with the men of Africa not to ritually castrate African women by cutting off their clitori are seen as much *more* sexually inhibited than the Africans who insisted that leaving the clitori intact would make the women sexually insatiable. White hipsters need a black man with an outrageously oppressive line on women to voice all the unpleasant, peasant fears they dare not air for fear of being bayonetted by their white feminist girlfriends.

If an African searches for your clitoris, he doesn't want to stimulate it – he wants to cut it off. Black sex was a slippery slope in the Seventies, and the black men who were its representatives on earth grew increasingly grotesque. Mr Poitier had rarely mentioned S.E.X., but one look at him was enough to provoke everlasting lust. The early years of the Seventies were played out against a soundtrack of Barry White and Sly Stone, the Laurel and Hardy of the Pecker Order, who though they boasted ceaselessly about their sexual capacities and made messy suggestions (Barry White: 'Take off your brassière, my dear . . .' – yuk!) were far too physically unappetizing to make the white man turn in the grave he called a matrimonial bed. And thus began the sexual deactivating process that would eventually serve up the dainty lukewarm dishes of Prince and Michael Jackson to an unsuspecting world.

In the Seventies there were blacks willing to defuse the bomb of black sexuality not only covertly, through careers of capering, but through direct hit ridicule. Jokes about the sexual competence of WASPs or any other ethnic groups had never before made anyone big in Vegas but America took to jokes against the erstwhile sex machine demons of their worst dreams like halibuts to H_2O: Richard Pryor's public puncturing of the black man's fifth column – 'We can't do it all night – sheeit, man, I can do it for two minutes and then I need eight hours sleep and a bowl of Wheaties!' –and Millie Jackson's harangues of a black boyfriend whose bravado is matched only by his sexual conservatism (she paints a vivid word picture of a man who balks at every conceivable sexual delicacy asked of him rather like a horse refusing each and every jump; from 'hung like a horse' to hung-up like a horse) were particularly popular. Miss Jackson even took her act to Sun City – the so-called 'mixed race' entertainment annexe of South Africa, where inter-racial brotherly love takes the shape of white men buying black women, where she was a wow. She would be, wouldn't she?

The black male visible achiever of the Eighties is not tall, dark and toothsome, like Poitier/Panther; he is effeminate – Prince, the black Tiny Tim – or celibate – Michael Jackson – or plain bland and uncharismatic – Eddie Murphy, the black Bob Hope. He is as sexless as the white man always dreamed he would be.

If the men are toys, boys or bores, the women are tarts, freaks or Mammies. In the most treacherous joke ever played on one oppressed minority by another, women like Eartha Kitt, Grace Jones and the Weather Girls became popular – with friends like that . . . – in the gay nightclubs of the metropolis in the Boystown Eighties because they made as large as life and twice as ugly all that gay men fear most about women: that they are grotesque, insatiable, castrating. Donna Summer's career of Godfearing soliciting – surely she is the singing patron saint of Hookers For Jesus – started big in the fistfucking parlours of solitary, sex-crazed gay America, where the boys pursued their orgasm fix to the coming-by-numbers of 'Love To Love You Baby'; the female (black) orgasm as a camp parody of the Real – white male – Things. When Donna Summer came out of the nightclub-closet and into the big marketplace, it was as the Sunset Strip strumpet of 'Bad Girls'; the only occasion on which a female singer – a very capable one, too – had been pushed as a prostitute in order to move units. When Donna Summer cracked in the Eighties, found God and de-nounced homosexuality – 'AIDS is a punishment from the Lord', people were shocked . . .

122

While white girls played at being men and virgins, black women pretended to be whores. Even Tina Turner – making her comeback in 1984 after years of working for and hiding from her husband Ike, the man behind the wanton image (microphone fellating and all) which caused white college-educated critics to hail her as the embodiment of untramelled, untamed female sexuality positively *revelling* in its power and freedom; in fact she lived in terror of the man and was kept in thrall by blackmail and violence just as sorely and sordidly as any cowed and mousey smalltown housewife – presented herself as a peepshow employee on the 1984 album 'Private Dancer'; and Tina Turner is forty-eight. Privately an abstemious Buddhist she, as Donna Summer once did, panders to the perverted and still pervasive myth that black women are more sexual than other women, *more animal* – the philosophy that once justified plantation rape. Having *had* more sex, because you could not lock your door, because you were someone's property, does not mean you *liked* it more; victimization does not equal appetite.

A schizoid cocktail of God, Mammon and faked orgasms masking soul on ice have led an endless, shameless soft parade of black entertainers to lend their support to Ronald Reagan, possibly the most stupid and useless American president of the lot, and whose policies have brought back the workhouses and food parcels of which blacks are the main beneficiaries. Prince, Summer, Eartha Kitt, James Brown, Ray Charles; they are not Uncle Toms, but Uncle Ron's. Born Again Republicanism is the hair-straightener of the 1980s. The glamorous, beautiful, brilliant blacks of the late Sixties and early Seventies – Ross, Poitier, Ali, Warwick, Wonder – were solid Democrat; their massive success never once came near buying them off, dazzling them like a necklace of glass beads once dazzled naive natives, and they didn't drone on about de Lawd endlessly either (though admittedly Ali put Allah *uber alles*; still, his Allah was a god who put him at *odds* with American society, not firmly in the mainstream of it). 'Our progress has never depended upon the President or Congress . . . it has always depended on the action of black people and the power of God,' said Andrew Young in 1982. The tragic dichotomy is that belief in the power of God more often than not makes black people completely inactive, and that belief in the power of prayer blanks out any belief in their potential for powerful action; castrated by Christ. Perhaps the story of blacks in America is so sad that it can only be countenanced through the stained glass window-coloured glasses of God's will; but what it amounts to is the existence of massive pockets of docility and laziness among the American black community, docility and laziness enough to make George Wallace come in his wheelchair – see Jesse Jackson's long hard 1980 state to state slog just to get the blacks to *register* to vote – *again*.

Inevitably gospel music itself, the cry of the powerless black calling on God to take him from this mortal coil and on to his mansion in the sky – a suicide note made song – underwent a revival in the Eighties, and the righteous retards who sang it were patronized by white athiest hipsters: like the Thirties Vassar pseuds who would advise each other, 'Read the Bible – for its style', the dilettante using the deadly serious chronic culture of the underclass as a *garnish* to their precious little lives, like a glorified cocktail cherry. It was around this time that Marvin Gaye was shot by his father, a preacher.

In Marvin Gaye the clash of the carnal and the Christian caused carnage. In the later years of his life, his pursuit of sensual gratification – the appetite for which was revealed so blatantly and beautifully in his early Seventies work – ' "Let's Get It On",' said my young middle-class brother-in-law nostalgically, 'I always used to put that on when I had a working-class girl on the sofa – and it always worked' – and his religious upbringing twisted him into mental pretzels which he could not make head or tail of. The interviews he gave veered frantically from boasting about his sexual exploits to warning that God was set to destroy Mankind because of his badness; this confusion led him to mind-lulling euphorics and narcotics, and led his father to kill him – because of his badness. When white aesthete atheists talk in awed voices of the priceless religious heritage of the American blacks, and the way this allows them to make such FANTASTIC music – God forbid Whitey should go without a part of the soundtrack to his all-important life – they do not consider what a terrible, almost tangible oppressor religion has been, and what terrible, mortal damage it has sustained upon the fighting spirit of the American black. God waits at every turning for his American black sheep, telling them to turn the other cheek, use the other entrance, wait for the other life. He pats their heads in their poverty and pats their backs when they're in the money, he dulls their pain – and therefore their anger – when they're down and turns their heads when they're up. Some hide, and some buy guns, and some read Mao, but he gets them all in the end; even Seale and Newton ended up *voluntarily* in jails helping blacks to find comfort in his fairy stories.

Marvin Gaye's God was a jealous God, and when he could not get Marvin Gaye Junior's undivided attention he got Marvin Gaye Senior to kill his son, just like he had dared Abraham. But he has no cause for complaint, and no need to feel he is playing gooseberry when it comes to another of his Motown-honed disciples: Michael Jackson, celibate and asexual, neither drinking, smoking or doping, talking of one day maybe *adopting* children. Tales of homosexuality and even hermaphroditism have been rife in the American scandal sheets but the truth is probably merely that Mr Jackson is neither fish, fowl nor fruit, just a man driven half mad by the conflicting demands of God and Mammon and choosing to spend his recreation in that safe babyplace beyond the procreation game.

He is a Jehovah's Witness, dedicated to the point of risking discovery; on public holidays, disguised in all manner of facial hair, he is in the habit of taking planes into the Mid-West heartland and knocking on doors in the well-known and annoying JW crusade to convert the homespun heathen. (Considering the Witness ban on blood transfusions, it would be interesting to see if they ever let this devout little billion dollar baby die rather than receive one.) Nevertheless, despite MJ's doing for the Jehovah's Witnesses what the Osmond Bros did for the Mormons – i.e. making it clear once more that the Jews have all the best tunes – his church have spoken out against his interest in things that do the Bump in the night (see the 'Thriller' video – In Cold Ketchup) which they foolishly perceive as sex-crazed Satanism rather than a child's fascination with the very things that scare him (i.e. girls and ghosts), while the mad black Muslim Louis Farrakhan has spoken out against his high voice and his even higher Panstik threshold because of the rather ambidextrous example it presents to all the young black dudes – you can't make a clenched fist with a limp wrist.

Not surprising Mr Jackson has used his millions – he was Number One at the age of eleven: public property before he had pubic hair: 1979's 'Off The Wall' sold eight million copies and has been credited with raising a tired and emotional record industry from its knees; 'Thriller', in 1982, sold more than thirty million copies – at times a million per week – won eight Grammy awards and pulled CBS Records into the black; the Jacksons' Victory Tour, the biggest tour in history, grossed one hundred million dollars (a minimum order of one hundred and twenty dollars' worth of tickets guaranteed an eighty per cent white audience) – to create a *very* well-protected environment for himself. The photo-electric detectors, Dobermanns and bullet-proof shower stalls of his neighbours are not all he needs to put between the world, its envious handguns and his precious self; he needs a soft cell, a playpen filled with toys and leisure technology, children and his mother, animals (llamas, boa constrictors, swans, fawns) and showroom dummies – 'They are the friends I never had.' A hybrid of Howard Hughes and Peter Pan, his eyes have been widened and his nose has been trimmed – a small nose and large eyes being essential ingredients of a child's face; he looks younger at twenty-six than he did at sixteen – and he wears green contact lenses and a 'magic' sequinned glove for good luck.

In conversation Michael Jackson uses the word 'magic' as often as the Panthers using 'mothafucka', and the choice of word is just as irritating. His basic problem is that he has the same view of childhood as the richer Victorians had; as a time that should be free of knowledge of all known adult pursuits – sex and work for two. He started touring at an age when most children are starting school, travelling around the grimy city of Gary, Indiana, and the surrounding Mid-West crammed into his father's Volkswagen with four brothers and two sisters – once on the same bill as a stripper; the cardinal childhood sins of sex and work combined – sometimes not going to bed until 5 a.m., rising after a couple of hours to put in a full day at school. Of course, had he not bothered with this rigorous routine he would quite likely be slaving over a hot steel press today; but no matter, as a true American he thinks he has a God-given right to Have It All – the early start that enabled him to be a millionaire before he could vote *plus* the Tom Sawyer childhood when all you had to worry about was breaking windows rather than breaking even. In England entertainers use heavy religious commitment as a veil over their reluctance to sleep with the opposite sex – 'Why don't you have a girlfriend?' 'I'm a Christian.' 'Oh, I see' – but in America they use religion as a Born Again sheepdip to cleanse past pillow pranks from the record – see Little Richard and a repentant cast of thousands – or, as in Michael Jackson's case, they use religious abstinence as an excuse not to grow up and get . . . married, divorced . . . *messy*.

Michael Jackson is harmless enough – that's why he's so popular – but he is not a big talent, let alone a big brain, and his attempts to recreate the perfect Disneyland childhood sometimes seem in danger of driving him mad. In 1982 he was asked to sing the theme song for the ET Storybook Album, but identified so strongly with the short, stretch-marked one that he asked Steven Spielberg if he could read the narrative. When there was a sad bit – sad bits being about as scarce as full stops – he would break down and cry. Said Steven Spielberg, obviously batting for the Norman Mailer–Jack Abbott Award For The Greatest Benefit Of The Doubt Given, 'He's sort of like a fawn in a burning forest.' (The Patience Strong Award For Stark Modern Prose, too.) 'It's a nice place where Michael comes from. I wish we could all spend some time in his world.'

The padded cell?

Michael Jackson does not get along well with his father, whose lifestyle – Mr Joe Jackson wears a brown leather jacket and left Mrs Jackson for a younger woman, both highly reprehensible actions – he disapproves of (The Marvin Gaye Story in reverse) and does not feel at ease with his brothers, who he dwarfs. Unlike Prince – the Jayne Mansfield to M.J.'s Marilyn; the short, stacked, souped-up sex cartoon parody of the mixed up megawaif prototype – who surrounds himself with pretty unknowns for pets and protégées, Michael Jackson knows that it's a small world in that tax bracket – a small world if you can afford it. His friends are the only people he can trust not to eat him alive – showroom dummies, and humans who pass the waxwork fame acid test: Hepburn, Astaire, McCartney, Ross, Fonda ('She teaches me all kinds of stuff' – from cheerleader to the Black Panthers to cheerleader for the black pussycat) – beings whose surnames are akin to brand names, they are so famous.

In the late Seventies, Michael Jackson was seen with Tatum O'Neal, the late childstar. Her cack-handed come-on to him provided him with the saddest story – even sadder than 'I LOVE TO FORGET' or 'I SIT IN MY ROOM SOMETIMES AND CRY' – M.J. ever told. 'She invited me to join her at Hugh Hefner's house to watch *Roots* on video tape. She got sort of bored, so we went outside and got into the jacuzzi.' J'ACUZZI! The memory of slavery had faded so fatally that a movie brat could use the representation of it as buckbait, freeze frame when the story was slow and jump into the jacuzzi without ever offending the black quarry. The racial memory of other black stars is equally pitiful: Mr T, the ex-All-American Dwarf-Hurling Champion who now features in *The A-Team*, claims that he spends two hours every morning putting on his weighty collection of gold chain jewellery 'to remind myself that my ancestors were slaves' (I've heard of some weak excuses for wearing medallions) while Eddie Murphy's considered analysis of the black experience goes thus; 'Shit, man. If I was a motherfuckin' slave, fuck that shit, man. Fuck that. I woulda said: "Yo', man, suck my dick, master, suck my motherfuckin' dick."' Mr Murphy's tender years and tough life do not come close to excusing his insensate ignorance.

Compared to the ever-present, prominent position the Holocaust holds in the collective memory of America and European Jews, slavery is gentle on the mind of the American black, never clamouring for attention or revenge or even reparations. White American racists know this, and

128

none of them has bothered to put out a pamphlet claiming that slavery never happened, as has been tried with reference to the Holocaust. Indeed, if such an idea is ever promoted it is likely to be by a rich Republican black urging his less fortunate brothers to 'be positive' – a.k.a., eat shit with a smile.

The stolid solid citizenship of the new Negro, the acceptance of deceit, injustice and the American way and the belief that America is the least worst place to be black must stem to some extent from the state Africa is in. Even accepting that the continent has been milked and manipulated ever since it was a twinkle in Antonio Gonsalves' telescope, it really cannot blame the white world for the fact that Bokassa fed his dogs with the flesh of his enemies any more than Britain can blame Rome – who colonized, enslaved and traded in Britons – for the glue-sniffing craze.

No black really wants to go back to Africa any more – there are already five million refugees there, for a start. Eldridge Cleaver, who fled there in the Seventies, returned in the Eighties to face jail in America rather than continue life as a free black man in Africa. (He, of course, became a Born Again Christian Republican and went on to produce a soul food cook book and a line of trousers – with a special fall-down mechanism for easy rape access, possibly.) In the Sixties, when black American interest in Africa was greatest, much of the continent was still held by the European colonizers and thus could be seen as the setting of several clearcut battles between the forces of light (the blacks) and darkness (the whites). But now, with the exception of South Africa, the continent belongs to blacks; and they have shown themselves every bit as capable of cruelty, corruption, racism (the expulsion of Asians in the Seventies; the expulsion of more than a million Ghanaians from Nigeria in 1983), silly bickering (incessant civil wars), censorship (in Kenya even *Das Kapital* is banned) and general atrocities – everyone knows now that black African dictators are just as ready, willing and able to kill black schoolchildren as whites in Selma, Alabama and South Africa – as their former rulers. This is why American blacks look to Lionel Richie rather than Lesotho for leadership and inspiration; because the African Dream has proved to be even more bankrupt than the American one.

Watching the USA For Africa singers perform 'We Are the World' to raise money for the relief of famine in Ethiopia, it was chastening to realize that a good three quarters of these wonderfully wealthy beings were black. For them, slavery had proved an unqualified success, the greatest career opportunity possible; glowing with good living, virtue and vitamins, Richie, Ross, Wonder, Warwick and the rest raised their voices for the benefit of those who had been unlucky enough to miss the boat – or rather the slave ship.

Despite what certain impatient dogmatists insist, it is much better if people are overfed than starved. No one wants the American blacks to go shoeless to show their solidarity with the people they left behind, and of course it is wonderful if they can get as large a slice of the American pie as possible. But it is a fact that there is smart money and spare change, even if the coins you earn for your antics add up to millions; there is clever success and dumb success. The successful blacks of the Sixties looked like gods; the successful blacks of the Eighties look like geeks. The successful blacks of the Sixties were sexy, sentient, sophisticated monarchs; the successful blacks of the Eighties are jesters.

In fact, the New Minstrelism is upon us, *'We are the world, we are the children'*, sing USA For Africa, and they highlight an American black crisis as well as an African one. To be a successful black entertainer today you must make sure that you stay in a pre-consciousness state of self-awareness, conscious neither of your colour nor the context in which it exists. It is this second childhood which enables blacks to support Ronald Reagan, this colour blindness which leads Prince and Michael Jackson to copious use of the heavy metal guitar – the whitest, most unsensual ingredient of postwar popular music. 'Boy' was for a long time the easiest way in which a white man, however stupid and ugly, could cut a black man, however clever and handsome, down to size; these days, blacks come ready shrunk, by their own hand. Sidney Poitier insisted on being called MR Tibbs (the name of Michael Jackson's sheep); but

Prince, a man in his late twenties, calls himself 'the Kid' in the autobiographical *Purple Rain*.

The latest and most damning development – or rather regression – in the infantilization of the American black is the graffiti/skipping/scratching/rapping/bodypopping/ breakdancing boom of the Eighties. Big black babies scribbling, spinning, singing mutated nursery rhymes are applauded by white artscum – '*He can write his name! He can jump a rope! He can make words rhyme!*' – as though they were dogs walking on their hind legs, simply for performing the most banal of actions. And, of course, they lower their horizons and standards accordingly.

Subway train and storefront graffiti, perhaps the most destructive and objectionable aspect of the New Minstrelism, started in the early Seventies amongst the teenage boys of black and Hispanic New York City but became the stuff Sunday supplements are made of in the Eighties as practised by adult men – men who had never moved on beyond the vapid vandalism of their bored schooldays. These profoundly retarded creatures – who call themselves things like 'President of the Death Squad' – steal out in the middle of the night and pick their way along the electric subway track – many have been mercifully put out of their misery this way – to spray their fanciful adopted names endlessly over the trains; the size of some of these masterpieces means they can take up to twelve hours to hone to perfection, and many of these young masters have been hit by moving trains while in the throes of creative genius. Defective spray cans sometimes explode in their faces, maiming them for life.

'To go over', to write over another's graffiti, is 'to disrespect'; this is the cause of much of the urban gang warfare. To 'bomb' is to write your name, to 'kill' is to write excessively while the recognized best at such scribbling is the 'king'. Kill, bomb, king: the inflated terms of war and glory only serve to make these illiterate child-adults more pathetic. What sort of starved mind can see 'respect' and rebellion in terms of a paintspray, or say, as Phase 2 did, 'The roots of graffiti are togetherness and the unity of the masses'? The missing link is alive and well and living in the South Bronx.

Of course, these wretches are patronized and encouraged like crazy by the white Eastern art establishment; the esperanto of graffiti is where the most fearful of whites meets the most harmless of blacks and STILL gets a thrill, simply because it's technically *illegal*. That illegal acts are not necessarily revolutionary, worthy or exciting has still not sunk in with the more sheltered sectors of society; especially with those people who need never get any closer to a paint-wrecked subway train than this month's coffee table art book.

Black graffiteers get to do sets for Twyla Tharpe and appear in films like *Wildstyle*, but the only mogul of messiness is a spindly, bespectacled white man, an ex-art student in his late twenties who sells his graffiti paintings for six figure sums, and talks about 'the kids' a lot, as unattractive, ageing ex-art students are prone to do. The nearest he gets to the kids these days, though, is his seventeen-year-old black assistant, who flexes the pecs and holds the master's cans. Graffiti eventually became so respectable that in April of 1985 a young New York scribbler called 'Brim' was flown in by the Greater London Council to give graffiti workshops.

Old Jewish Hollywood showed blacks in the context of white society – oppressed, struggling, winning and losing. The black equivalent of the beach party films which are now so ubiquitous – *Breakdance, Electric Boogaloo* (in which the dancers move as if they had an electric current going through them – if *only*) and all – feature young men and women who are happy as sandboys and, as Anthony Denselow so cleverly said, 'live in ghettoes furnished by Habitat'. Like the video for 'Hello', in which the girl interest was blind, black and a student, *and lived in a penthouse*, they are set somewhere over the rainbow with an impressive disregard for living conditions on this planet.

The protaganists' refusal to recognize that being black is a handicap in America is matched only by their refusal to perceive that there might be some other road to fame and fortune other than clowning, grinning and spinning on your shoulders. These films could be funded by and set in Sun City, so closely do they conform to the South African ideal of black destiny: born to sing, dance and live separately.

Beat Street made five million dollars in three days – but then trends do. There is no reason why these young people should not have their fifteen minutes like the rest of us. The sad thing is that unlike the great black entertainers of the past, so little is *asked* of these young people that there is no chance at all that they can strive and thrive the way those from Robeson to Ross did; when their time is up these assorted graffiteers, skippers, scratchers, rappers, body-poppers and breakdancers will fall by the wayside like so many human hula hoops – living, breathing, obsolescent gimmicks. They will go back to the streets they were sucked up from in the first place, older, unskilled and embittered, and they will live off the streets and their glory stories until they get caught. They will go from their playpens to their jails, and never know what it was like to be free.

America really never was a melting pot; just a huge patchwork of ghettos, all colours and creeds neatly and discreetly divided and programmed young for the life they can expect. American Negroes still live short, brutal and unrewarded lives – a black male between the ages of fifteen and thirty-four is more likely to be murdered than to die from any other cause (unlike the white man, who will die in a motor accident). Yet they do seem to feel that in some way they have *arrived*; perhaps this has something to do with the huge Hispanic immigration wave which started in the Seventies and continues to this day, and which has given the blacks a people even poorer and less integrated than themselves to look down on – there being no tonic like the troubles of others. There is one black astronaut, one black country singer, one black *Dynasty* character, so theoretically this means anyone can do it; broken by tokens.

They have lost themselves, and worse still they have let themselves go; from Ali saying he would not kill yellow men for white men to Prince saying Reagan has 'balls' (yes, where his brain should be); from The Supremes dedicating 'Stop! In the Name of Love' 'to President Nixon, with reference to the war in Vietnam' to Grace Jones naked, caged and snarling for the camera of her white Svengali; from Paul Robeson, the day Mao won, singing the Red Chinese National Anthem phonetically from a scrap of paper, the happiness shining out of him, to Richard Pryor running through the streets of Bel Air with his face on fire from freebasing, a KKK wet dream; from John Carlos on the Olympic winners' podium with his head bowed and one black-gloved fist thrust into the Mexico City sky all through 'The Star Spangled Banner' – three minutes that shook the satellited world with the awareness of black pride – to Ed Moses encouraging the American black runners into a *huddle* before they get on the blocks, to *pray*. By 1977 'Burn Baby Burn' was not a cry of vengeance ricocheting around the flaming ghettos but a song by the Trammps strobing around the discos, and pride was narcissism, and American blacks were Negroes again. They entered the twentieth century with the most potent weapon in the world – organization. The only organization they will leave the century with is the Michael Jackson Fan Club.

Damaged Gods

In 1985, Alan Bleasdale — 'the most popular writer since Dickens' said John Mortimer — presented a play at the aptly named Phoenix Theatre concerning the later life of the sneer that ate the world — and anything else it could get its hands on — Elvis Presley. During rehearsals he had sent a copy of the biography by Albert Goldman — the Simon Wiesenthal of showbusiness — to the actor who was to play Elvis, with a note:

CONTAINS MANY FACTS BUT LITTLE TRUTH. BEWARE. CONTACT WITH THIS MATERIAL CAN BE FATAL.

Goldman's book, written over many years, came from practically every living source close to the ageing Presley. Immensely touching, it revealed sides of the unappetizing Mr P previously unknown to (news)man — the child who gave away his toys, the grotesquely distended idol who nevertheless got down on his knees to propose marriage to his last Tennessee girlfriend, Ginger Alden, stating that he had been all around the world but that he had never expected to find something so precious in his own backyard.

It also showed him to be a bully, a racist, a drug addict, a glutton and a neurotic, so morbidly attached to the idea of Mother that he could not sleep with his own wife after she had had their baby.

It was ironic that Alan Bleasdale, famous for the definitive fictional portrait of the ugliness of life in monetarist Eighties Britain, could not swallow the definitive factual portrait of the ugliness of life at the top of the

135

bracket. BEWARE – CONTACT WITH THE TRUTH CAN BE FATAL. You can do anything – but don't step on my blue sweet dreams.

Elvis Presley was the final image of the twentieth-century entertainer, the American Success – a man endlessly rich, who had everything money could buy, and who had taken so many tranquillizing drugs in the last years of his life that he could no longer control his insides but lay there on his vast revolving bed wearing huge improvised nappies made of bath towels. Alan Bleasdale, revered for showing life *as it is at its worst*, was enraged by the portrayal of his hero – whom he describes as the twentieth century's only Greek God – AS HE WAS: a fat man instead of a snake-hipped deity. The ordinary people of Liverpool could be shown genital warts and all; the Greek God, on the other hand, must be allowed to keep his dignity. But the lies told about the healing power of showbusiness success have caused just as much heartbreak as the lies told about the harmless effect of prolonged unemployment on Liverpool navvies ever did.

In writing a play to defend his hero's reputation, Alan Bleasdale, a man of wealth and taste, was reacting from the same impulse that caused another Elvis Presley fan to have plastic surgery in order to look like the twin of his idol; that causes a young boy in Brighton to keep the debris from Paul Daniels' nose in a matchbox; that caused a woman to jump in front of Frank Sinatra's car shouting 'Run me over, Frankie!'; that caused cripples at Beatles shows to beg to be touched by the four giants among men; that caused the bouncers at Xenon in New York to become hysterical at its opening and shriek 'Celebrities! Only celebrities!'; that caused Mark Chapman to love John Lennon so much that he killed him so that their names would be linked together for ever like Romeo and Juliet, like John and Lee Harvey, like legendary lovers. The impulse that leads the simple soul to believe in the benediction of the neon lights, the purging power of the roar of the crowd and the scream of the sirens, and the city sort of love – the worship of the Entertainer.

Man has always had a need to divert himself from his one and only life; to see entertainment as some Reaganite–

Thatcherite plot to divert the workers of the world from their true aims (you have nothing to lose but your *Dallas*) is silly. Even before the Trivia Mafia gained control of the television channels and Fleet Street decided to devote its resources to churning out daily fun magazines – things resembling the stained sheets of the famous rather than the news sheets of the citizen – the man in the field looked to bear-baiting and cock-fighting to divert him from his measly lot; he used his leisure time not to plot sedition but to crouch by his hearth scaring his friends with vampire stories. Long before Hammer Films gave it to him, he needed the vampire.

WE NEED THE VAMPIRE. To see the entertainment system as a capitalist conspiracy is madness; yet there is something taking place, something big and seething, in which the desire to be diverted occasionally is becoming a full-blown obsession with escape through entertainment. In the Seventies, American teachers reported that previously promising college students had started to drop out of their classes in order to be able to follow the born-again torrid daytime soap operas – people sacrificing real lives because the fictional lives of others seemed more immediately, vitally important. As the world opens up and gets bigger, we close up and feel smaller, and turn our troubled minds and stomachs from the torments of factual continents to the quarrels of fictional streets; as the world becomes a global village, we become global village idiots, sleepwalking through a life where our best friends are soap opera characters – and our leaders are, too.

We are heading towards a time when real life will only be understood through entertainment – the working class through *Coronation Street*, women's interests through *The Women's Room*, the Second World War through *Winds of War*, slavery through *Roots*. Information not presented as entertainment will not be absorbed – the rise of 'faction' shows this. A people who cannot digest anything but fiction – the strained babyfood of communications – and who do not believe, like Mr Bleasdale, that facts and truth are the same, are in danger of mass stupidity – of passing on to their children a world divided strictly into entertainers and audiences, in which the bringer of boring knowledge will not be welcome at all.

The celebrity sausage machine has been speeded up; from the new rash of Make It youth films (making it in youth films used to refer to sex – now it refers to FAME) to the breaking down of old industry – expendable little things like coal and steel – in favour of 'leisure technology'. Leisure, entertainment, fame: in the Eighties they became our liberty, equality and fraternity. Britain, as the favoured offshore island of the USA, was commissioned not to produce lowly bananas or orphans but ENTERTAIN-MENT; Tom Wolfe wrote of the day Britain would be one big theme park, and all its citizens 'Viddies' – characters in videos made for American consumption. When it was suggested in 1985 that Battersea Power Station be made into a leisure park, it begged a bitter pun. Great Britain, 1985: all leisure and no power.

Entertainment is *the* business of the later half of the twentieth century, as the motor car was the business of the first half and the railroad the business of the later half of the last century. Man wanted to MOVE; and after a hundred years of getting to the Promised Land, the future, found it lacking and employed a time machine to take him back to the past. People wonder that H.G. Wells got it wrong for once, and imagined some scientific gadget that never actually happened – but we have a time machine in every sitting room. People spend much more diversion from their lives than they do on either health or warfare; however, they do make rich forces which hasten their deaths (cigarette and alcohol manufacturers, drug dealers) rather than those who preserve their lives. But there is nothing like a decoy; last year a nurse could have expected to earn around £6000 while Prince, the Paisley Ponce, earned thirty-two million pounds.

The human spirit being the perverse thing it is, some players of the fame game, both active and passive, display spirit. When twelve young aspiring actors, men and women, black and white, agreed to *live* in a huge billboard overlooking Sunset Strip, ostensibly to promote a new piece of flashing jewellery called 'The Winkie' but actually to further their careers – the longest survivor, recalling the dance marathons of the Thirties, was promised a new car, a promotional trip to New York City and a screen test with a prominent film studio — at the start of 1985, prissy English writers declared it to be a symptom of Reaganism, the New Mean Chic Revival Medicine Show, the unacceptable butt of naked ambition and a host of other silly and amock-alyptic things. The American National Anthem *had* been played before the winkers ascended to the great billboard in the sky, after all, and mistakes are made. But after one night three of the actresses deserted their post and the next day the remaining nine had UNIONIZED and were demanding cars and screen tests for all. Far from illustrating the naked, make-it, cut-throat drive of Eighties America as billed, the National Union of Winkie Wearers struck the biggest blow for American altriuism in the workplace since the Wobblies — who come to think of it also sound like a bunch of hoofers promoting jewellery in a billboard over Sunset Strip.

Clark Gable, when approached by drooling female fans in the Fifties, would take out his false teeth, chatter them in his palm and ask his fans how they could possibly love such a disgusting old man. The Princess of Wales, that poor prisoner of warmth who has been trumpeted into the nation's consciousness by the Fleet Street fanzines as a national amalgam of Marilyn and the Madonna, was on the cover of the mousewife magazines as their circulation plunged all through the mid-Eighties, copious use of her blush and bangs not stopping the defection to the diet journals — obviously thousands of women preferred to have a stab at being their own heroines, despite what the monarchy-mooning press told them. To Una Merkel in 1933, after requesting a signed autograph, a fan wrote back 'Do not send picture. Decided I don't want it.' The actress telegrammed her, 'Picture is sent. You'll take it and like it.'

But on the whole, fame is a game that attracts the unbalanced on both sides. The Hollywood Sign is the alternative Statue of Liberty, hungry for losers, loners, introverts and misfits to grind down and recycle as brand new born-again giant-sized loved ones — fame is Nature's way of saying sorry. The reason why so many entertainers end up stiff after last rites of Seconal has probably less to do with entertainment MAKING people crazy than with neurotics being attracted to it in the first place, eager to obliterate the hated self in a white hot other. What makes a star a star is not that 'indefinable something extra' the low-browed girls and high-heeled boys talk about in reverent, quiet-in-the-library murmurs – what makes a star a star is that indefinable something MISSING. As that benign if jaded Womble scavenger of Manhattan's flotsam and jetset Andy Warhol once said of his cracked actors, the scared shadows of young Americans he made over into Underground film stars (Underground films are so called, incidentally, because they are about as interesting as riding the Tube in the rush hour), when accused of 'exploitation': 'I don't know what all the fuss is about. I didn't take babies with perfect chemicals and mess them up.' He salvaged what had already been damaged beyond repair and gave it a reason to stick around in this penny-ante world for a few frames more. The same goes for showbiz proper – only bigger, with flashbulbs on.

So great is the healing power of the celluloid tourniquet that a man like Sylvester Stallone – who though of draft age and physical condition acted as athletics coach in a Swiss private school during the American war against Vietnam – can be reborn as Rambo, the 'pure killing machine' in the eyes of the American people, the dead French poet with the 46-inch chest who returns to Vietnam to search for his bosom buddy the brilliant but flawed Private Verlaine in the latest loud lullaby – also written and conceived by the immaculate Sly – to help America sleep safely at night. It grossed over 75 million dollars in three days, and grossed out millions more Europeans. Posters of Sly-Rambo hang in the windows of US Army recruitment offices – the most bosomy soldier boy's pin-up since Rita Hayworth. Slambo is surely the next President of the United States, with a war record – all mouth and megabucks – that even Ronald Reagan would be proud to call his own.

Such solid proof of adoration as Prince's thirty-two million smackers per annum, citizens putting their money where their minds are, can easily have a destabilizing effect on an ego already cut free and cast adrift. Life having speeded up as it has, it is not unusual for a performer to go off his raspberry rocker not in the grey gardens of his decline and dotage, but at the peak of his youth and popularity. Fan worship is like some miracle cure which wipes out dowdy perspective and horse sense as instantly as spit on a griddle. I want to rule the world, says the beautiful but unexceptional Madonna (beauty being the commonest, most expendable, badly abused fertilizer of fame) when asked her ambition on an American talk show, whereas a more realistic goal might be to break even this time next year. Prince had been a household face for less than a year when his aides went before him to the film set where his friend Sheila Escovedo was working and handed out cards which told the crew DO NOT LOOK AT PRINCE. But they did, and he fled — a petulant Persephone for a modern Greek tragedy.

Stars, supposedly the most special and individual of people, all become one star at a certain point, like junkies become one junkie and can be predicted down to the last tiny track mark. Stars behave as the newspapers and some racial memory tells them stars behave: wearing dark glasses into nightclubs, refusing to be photographed after six solid months of working nine to five — nine at night to five in the morning, that is — on their exposure, bursting into tears for no apparent reason, sleeping with famous pushovers and showing amazement and disgust when their sheath size is revealed to a sniggering public, eating and drinking themselves silly, getting divorced, punching photographers, getting remarried to someone half their age and twice their height, trying suicide on for size, retiring to a health farm, being Born Again and making comebacks.

The broadly accepted showbiz scenario that sees stars as larger than life beings who brighten our drab lives by shedding their radiance upon us comes in for quite a bashing when you survey the entertainment marketplace. For every brilliant creature there are fifty plain chaps of both sexes who are popular just *because* they are unexceptional in every way. Their names and nationalities change, though they are often Irish, but their appeal is constant — The Call Of The Mild. They are chat show hosts and lachrymose lushes weeping into their pianos and comedians, but they are always similarly untalented and unthreatening, entirely reliant on the collaboration of their public. Being a fan of an entertainer of genius can be an unrewarding business – you can withdraw your support at a moment's notice and lack of it won't make your target any less of a genius. But if you are a fan of a hackstar, you have power – you and the others like you can stop listening/ laughing/buying and the glorified nonentity will have nothing left, for when he ceases to please he ceases to exist. People appreciate this feeling of vicarious power, and feel well disposed towards those who give it to them – which is why geniuses die penniless much more often than game show hosts.

'Fame' comes from the Latin for rumour, and the status of a celebrity is maintained by the modern jungle drums, the publicity machines, whose grip on good English is just as tenuous. It is quite well recognized that the untalented pursue fame while the talented evade it – the difference between Garbo and Tiny Tim, to be crass – but less acknowledged that publicity can actually foil and despoil and deactivate talent. When Farrah Fawcett left *Charlie's Angels* to make an intelligent, liberal, comedy thriller called *Somebody Killed Her Husband* she showed a light-handed, likeable comic talent similar to the young Carole Lombard's; but Rin Tin Tin might as well have played Lady Macbeth. Because of the widespread publicity the girl's hairstyle had received the film was panned, her performance deemed laughable rather than funny and the girl herself retired to off-off Broadway and Ryan O'Neal. In fifty years' time we will probably queue in front of art houses to see Farrah Fawcett retrospectives, but for the rest of her natural lifetime a Farrah Fawcett will mean a hairstyle, not an actress. The publicity men who came to praise her buried her.

While she was appearing off-off Broadway, a man who must have been the last Farrah Fawcett fan in captivity jumped up on the stage and grabbed the shorn actress. In the early years of the Eighties, Victoria Principal had a bullet-proof shower stall installed in her high security Hollywood house. After the killing of John Lennon, George Harrison had a house built on the Pacific island of Maui which was surrounded on three sides by jungle and on one side by a sheer drop to the jagged cliffs hundreds of miles below, in the shadow of the volcano Haleakala, where he spends most of his time. What makes a man eager to live under a volcano if it means he can escape the rest of his species? Nothing but the spectre of the Fan, whose name came from 'fanatic' and whose public image has mutated right the way back there. The Fan, who will literally love you to death.

It was the rise of the soap opera even more so than the occasional celebricide that caused the perception of the fan to shift from treat to trick to threat; the realization, just a joke at first but soon confirmed by the actors themselves, that many people who watched soap operas could not tell truth from fiction (perhaps, like Alan Bleasdale, they believe that truth and fact are not the same thing). No one really thought that Garbo was Camille; but the regularity and banality of the American daytime soap operas mimicked life for those in the regular, banal hinterlands of America. The stories are legion now about the actresses whose characters have considered − just considered − abortion, and have been spat on in the street by law-abiding citizens − of actors who play cripples whose legs are pinched and probed by curious fans. Soap actors receive letters offering love, marriage and, when all else fails, death. According to *Variety*, 10 per cent of all fan mail sent from within the USA comes from people with Polish names − another one in five Americans is illiterate, and not even aware that the names of actors come up on the screen at the end of their daily soap. Given these two frightening and vital statistics, it is not too surprising that ex-Mop Tops are fleeing to cliff tops like safety-conscious lemmings.

A harmless crush can become a clinical obsession when held a beat too long. The fan has no power over the performer but to destroy, and because of this he flexes his only working muscle frequently; in the witholding of affection, translated as consumption, and in the giving of threats and in the dealing of death. His impact is fiscal, fatal or not at all, whereas the impact of the star is incessant and nagging through the many media, like the ghost of an abandoned dream. The thin line between love and hate, between free will and fate, gradually disappears for the fan in the attic, lumping around his unacknowledged, unwanted love like an embarrassing erection all stressed up with nowhere to go; and the love turns into a weapon as he realizes he can never touch the one he wants, except with a bullet. More often than not it is no more than a paper chase, taking place in letters and locked diaries, but occasionally dreams come true. If a 'personality' is shorthand for someone famous, then the anonymous have no recognized personalities, and like all ciphers they can commit crimes against humanity − crimes against celebrity.

The fan who breaks on through to the place where fact and fiction are identical twins has achieved most fully the dream entertainment promises: escapism. The man who threatens the soap opera actress with love and then death because of her cathode canoodlings has escaped completely from reality − he is the success story of escapist entertainment, the mad aristocrat of the neurotic mass which always knows when it has had enough − the bourgeois failing.

Is there any such thing as harmless escapism? Perhaps only in cases of philanthropy, demonstrated most impressively by Live Aid, Fame For Famine, when people's desire to be diverted in the form of pop music helped solve a problem − which might not have become so serious, incidentally, if Westerners had been looking more at the Horn of Africa and less at the Texan Horn of Cornucopia. A world in which the affluent spend all their money on diversion from life is invariably a very frightening place for the poor. The kids of *Fame* can do a perky little song and dance routine about it not being important that you're black and underprivileged and at the bottom of the heap, you can always breakdance your way to the top, but the kids of famine cannot. The corpse at every christening, the mourner at every wedding, they cannot expect too much airtime; of course the death of Bobby Ewing (fictional) gets more coverage in the next day's papers than the death of a thousand Africans (factual). To a sleepwalking people, fearful of the shock of consciousness, Bobby Ewing was real in a way a thousand faceless Africans could never be.

Only at odd times − during a war, say − do people actually act as if their one life on earth is precious to them. The rest of the time they use a range and mixture of tranquillizers − entertainment, alcohol, art − to escape from it. Westerners on the whole seem to want neither to fully live nor fully die, but to hang in limbo, semi-conscious, hooked up to the life support machine in the corner – everyone knows the 1984 news story of the family who had to be forcibly moved from their flat as it burnt up around them; three generations spellbound by the new video nasty they had just acquired, oblivious to the fact that they were all set to star in one of their own. Most people in the West wish to sleepwalk through life with the minimum of fuss and bother, and entertainment provides them with people who will be witty and bitchy *for* them, commit adultery *for* them, kill and die *for* them, live *for* them. The more underprivileged the person, the older or poorer, the bigger will be the screen in the corner from which the ravishingly rich first families of fictional America (although the accusations that *Dynasty* and *Dallas* are 'unrealistic' compared to pessimistic Let's Pretends such as *Cathy Come Home* may be unrealistic themselves: America had 832,602 millionaires in 1984, growing at the rate of 9 per cent a year. The American Dream still has such power and is so hard to stifle because it actually comes true for so many people) point the glossily manicured finger at the grim lives and fatal failure of the surreally poor. This is the greatest aid the UnDead have, even more so than legally prescribed barbiturates.

Like prostitution, with which it shares many qualities – escape from real life and real people and real responsibility, one-way traffic, payment, parody: like bought sex, there is something sad and strange about bought entertainment. WHY can't you get it from your friends? Why can't you get it free? What's wrong with them? What's wrong with YOU? That people should have to go to people who don't know them for entertainment is as illogical as going to people who don't know them for sex. It is not surprising that many prostitutes call themselves 'actresses' – the demand for entertainment creates the supply rather than vice versa. The Audience, that many-mouthed hog, is as dominant fiscally as it is slavish emotionally, and the purveyors of entertainment must cut their creative cloth according to its whims. Cinemas and studios have closed down in their thousands since the advent of television, enabling people to be entertained in their own private padded cells rather than at set times and places, and continue to close now that video has made even TV look nannyish, video being the ultimate anarchic baby mode of entertainment technology – I'll watch soft porn and hard nasty till I scweam and scweam, until I'm sick, so there! Mr Zadora pours money into Mrs Zadora as though she were an exotic nationalized industry, but the waning power of Pia shows no sign of going into reverse. *Dallas*, often cited as *the* symbol of American cultural imperialism by excitable Left-wing Amockalypsists – all those Hitlers in Halstons and Simon Legrees in stetsons – has never knocked the wretched homegrown soap operas of Britain, most of Latin America and Japan (where it was taken off after six months, after never netting more than 4 per cent of the population) from the top spot in their own countries, despite the fact that an episode of *Dallas* costs $700,000 to make, that Victoria Principal's pedicurist gets more than all the cast of *Crossroads* put together, despite the fact that the domestic product is invariably composed of uglier actors and sets comprising one wardrobe, one coffee table and two doilies (optional). (As Brian Case once said of *Crossroads*, 'Everyone is always wearing housecoats, drinking cocoa and making things horrid.') Yet people prefer them – because they are less obviously foreign and fictional than *Dallas*, and easier to drown in, to take as gossip and gospel truth. They are easier to believe in, and be friends with. When the long-standing and long-suffering heroine Meg Richardson was written out of *Crossroads* after twenty years, the man who made the decision was threatened with death, and when the actress Noele Gordon died some months afterwards he was accused of 'killing Meg'. *Crossroads* lost around four million viewers after killing the carrot-coiffed commandant of Crossditz and trying to do a *Dallas* by importing a shoal of tough and tinted career girls, but by the autumn of 1985, despite the incessant sniping over the amount of 'American trash' being shown on British TV, the top fifteen programmes were English, nine of them soap operas. The many-mouthed hog doesn't know much about art, but it knows what it likes, and what it likes is what it gets.

The case for the entertainer as sacrificial young lion rather than agent of social control, fleetingly celebrated underdog rather than smug *ubermensch* is really rather strong. One might lean more towards the idea of modern American entertainment as wicked Reaganite blindfold if the major glamour figures of Hollywood did not still espouse liberal causes, as they always have – a much greater proportion of millionaire entertainers would seem to have social consciences than the man in the mezzanine on the whole. Rambos come and go, but Robert Redfords and Raquel Welches seem set to last for ever. Only Charlton Heston and the Osmonds turn out for Reagan rallies, and they are hardly the hottest properties in the Peoples Republic of Burbank.

Once again, the conspiracists might have a point about the promise of fame being the dangling carrot of capitalism if fame were really shown as the answer to all prayers and problems – but the divorces, depressions and early deaths of the prime products of the fame machine are an industry in themselves. Most people have probably seen more films about the sad life and death of Marilyn Monroe KILLED BY FAME! – no more than any young housewife in her early thirties dying alone from too many sleeping pills is KILLED BY ANONYMITY! – than they have seen films starring Marilyn Monroe. A celebrity marriage may make a nice headline for one morning – but a celebrity divorce may make a Hundred Days War, just the tonic the newsagent ordered. It is not unfair to say that civilians enjoy the *pain* of celebrities much more than their triumphs: it is probably the combination of bloodsport and worship, both such blind, fatalistic, primitive dark forces, that makes celebrity such a powerful religion. Don't kill me a son, kill me a STAR, says the jukebox Jehovah.

Similarly, the misfit, weirdo, idealist and downright nasty bastard has emerged as the hero of so many American entertainments that the process can hardly be accused of promoting the American Way. Hollywood has glamourized the misfit so often – from left and right, right down to Rambo who is permanently at odds with the big brass back home – that Oscar ceremonies often read like a Weirdos Convention.

In the Sixties the cocaine Communists – natural heirs to the limousine liberals – of Tinseltown demonstrated just how far beyond the mainstream, and just how far removed from ordinary people – film fans – they were by producing a string of films which had violent psychopaths as their heroes. That violent criminals are *not* rebels, but the warped policemen of poor communities – causing people to lock their doors, stay inside, live in fear – was lost on these butterflies; it is easy to canonize criminals when you have bodyguards. The craze culminated in the making of *Bonnie and Clyde*, in which two perfectly hideous and brutish murderers of eighteen people of 1934 were turned into two bona fide Beautiful People of 1967. 'They were young, beautiful and they killed people,' ran the film's advertising catchline.

It would be interesting to know if the Manson Gang of Death Valley, frequent guests at the parties on the cusp of glamour and gutter in the Hollywood of the late Sixties, saw the film and heard the slogan and thought of themselves in the same light when they killed the young movie actress Sharon Tate Polanski and six other people in the last summer of the Sixties. They were certainly no uglier than Bonnie and Clyde, although perfectly repellent. They were literally *not half as bad* – only seven deaths to eighteen. Yet no film would dare show them as sensitive, poetry-writing young beauties forced into their position by an unsympathetic society – Mark Chapman either – and if one did, Warren Beatty et cie would be appalled. Because Bonnie and Clyde – even their names were familiarized to make them sound like a groovy young married Sixties crooning couple: Bonnie and Clyde and Sonny and Cher – killed *ordinary people*, film *fans*, while Sharon Tate was a REAL PERSON, one of *them*, precious. After the Tate murders, the Hollywood brats showed less enthusiasm when it came to giving a makeover to the hideous psycho killers of American folklore and in the mid Seventies the same cocaine Communists were fond of employing the slogan DON'T BUY BOOKS BY CROOKS to blacklist the post-Watergate autobiography of Richard Nixon. But they had been buying something much worse for years – buying murderers' sweetest dreams of themselves.

If the fan's attitude to the star is ambiguous, love and hate mixed, the star's to the fan is less so. It is usually one of fear and contempt, varying in the measures of each. It is taken for granted that stars are friends only with other stars, the excuse most usually offered being that ordinary people might just want to know you for *what* you are, rather than *who* you are. This blandly proffered, blandly accepted justification alone shows depths of misanthropy and paranoia that, for starters, without even digging any deeper into the admittedly shallow star psyche, condemns the star irretrievably from his own mouth. Another reason, never admitted, is that stars tend to be the biggest groupies of all: see the shameless way that aged Thirties film stars flock to pay court to the young dark singers of our time; they lick the boots and kiss the feet of people only once removed – albeit by fame – from shining their shoes.

Although it fatally contradicts the myth of a happy human species 99 per cent of which is born to be entertained and 1 per cent to entertain, and everyone very happy with the arrangement thank you very much Miss Sharp, stars really do look down on those who have not been born famous, achieved fame or had fame thrust upon them. The famous are a breed beyond all creed or colour bars – Sammy Davis Jnr has more in common with John Wayne than with a black janitor who came from the same street, and so does Jane Fonda than with a badly paid union organizer on the Mississippi. When she presented the dying Il Duke with a special Oscar for his services to the motion picture industry, it was all Prodigal Commie smiles and choked sobs, principles and politics forgotten. Blood is thicker than napalm, after all. The famous blur beyond colour, class, creed, fact, fiction and job description, as when Henry Kissinger waddled across an episode of *Dynasty* as himself – 'Why, Henry, I haven't seen you since Portofino,' smirked Joan Collins' Alexis, and it all seemed as natural as bombing Cambodia when you're at war with Vietnam.

The famous marry fame, breed fame; and like any small, inbred race living in fear of their lives they suffer from acute xenophobia. They see the non-famous as a scuffling ant heap (although nothing could be more inelegantly scuffling than the spectacle of showbiz kids attempting to beat each other out for *this* part, *that* award and generally *make their pile*) from which they themselves escaped by the skin of their capped teeth. They dislike them because the celebrated were hardly ever the golden boys and girls of high school – everyone has seen the school photographs of every famous beauty from Garbo to Raquel showing the young goddess complete with double chin, spectacles and victimized eyes – and had plenty of long hot school's-out back-bedroom summers in which to nurse their lonely loathing of their contemptuous contemporaries as if it were a runt puppy made strong through undivided attention and patience. And they dislike fancifully named 'human-ity' because it really is an unedifying sight when seen from above, a monster gaping up at you composed of a million drooling mouths, prying eyes and grabbing hands, dis-gusting in the way a voyeur crossed with a coward is disgusting, scared to do anything but scream at YOU to walk the tightrope, urging the ringmaster to remove the safety net, to increase the all-important THRILL. When Elizabeth Taylor buried Mike Todd, film fans perched on tombstones eating popcorn, as though they were con-sumers of yet another Liz Taylor film. When she noticed this and became hysterical, the press treated the scene as though it was *she* who had behaved oddly.

'When you're a performer,' says Michael Jackson, 'people want everything. One asked me in front of every-one, "Do you go to the bathroom?" I was so embarrassed I didn't know what to say. I don't always trust myself with regular people.' (Perhaps he prefers constipated ones.) 'My idea of your average person is someone in a crowd who's running towards me trying to tear my clothes off.' (Of course, if Mr Jackson led a normal young man's life that would be the behaviour of his nearest and dearest, too.) 'It's a whole other life.' Some stars become as neurotic as their fans (Tony Schailer talking to *Smash Hits*: 'If I've got a problem, I'll talk to Francis Rossi as if he was in the room with me. It's got to the stage where they're just my life. If I lost my job, it wouldn't bother me. As long as I've got Status Quo, there's something worth carrying on for. I once met Francis . . . he shook my hand and my eyes filled with water. He said, "It's O.K., mate, don't worry about it." It was the best moment of my life so far.'), washing com-pulsively after being mobbed, becoming convinced that the cameras are trying to 'steal' their faces. (Perhaps they are.) They are obsessed with the fact that their fans 'want something' from them. Maybe they do. But these sensitive little artistes choose to forget that they want something from their fans – every red cent they can get. And when you set out to take people's money, by fair means or foul, with a crowbar or a comedy routine, when you set out to take the very stuff that keeps people from being human litter on the streets, selling yourself as though you were as essential to their lives as food and shelter, you must expect a violent response one way or another. If you would take something as important as their money, you must give something as important as your self.

The story of America is really the story of a succession of strange, sometimes almost certainly certifiable charismatics from Semple McPherson to McArthur to McCarthy to Manson to Moon who have inspired devotion from sections of American society – such as it is – sometimes tiny, sometimes huge, sometimes whole states or generations. I question whether 'American society' exists at all because in a country as sprawling and confused and diverse as the young USA was, the cult of the individual was forced on people in such a way that they would not think of themselves as members of non-American racial grouping but as American originals, as individual and unrepeatable as snowflakes – as opposed to the people of other nations who are seen as faceless blurs, things to be colonized and, showing resistance, killed. Such artificially individualized people are much more prone to the lure of the guru, the idol, the million Only Ways than the people of any legitimate society with a history of people's upheavals and mass movements – the Black Mass, to the Americans, for whom the Individual shines with a halo. America's hysterical fear of Communism stems not from any real fear of brutality or oppression – but from the fear of not being able to wear the sloganized T-shirt of your choice, of not being an all-important (literally) individual. This very special alone-ness, this fear of natural, historical, political groupings while self-imposed, illogical groupings – from Fan Club to Manson Family – are manifold and manic, is yet another of America's many unhelpful exports to a breathless, mindless white world.

But entertainment is really the least of modern America's ills. If people must worship, let them worship Madonna rather than McCarthy; if they must be diverted, let them be diverted by MTV rather than bear-baiting. Let the people of the American-speaking world, sensing their powerlessness which has made them as apathetic as poverty made their old world ancestors, distract themselves with the only things they feel they have power over – trends, fads, ENTERTAINMENTS. Let the political process itself become not a part of real cause and effect life but a *spectator sport*, full of actors and cowboys, as the vote goes down and the parapolitical entertainments – *Rambo 19* – go up. Let African villages continue to get cassette players before they get running water – who cares? Certainly not the inhabitants of the white world in the last quarter of the twentieth century, whose lives are reflected not in the achievements of nearest dearest but far stars, symbols, small conflicts and cultural sideshows; and where development is really and truly over, and only diversion is left.